GOD IS A MATCH-MAKER

Other books by Derek Prince

Biography:
Appointment in Jerusalem

Guides to the Life of Faith:
Faith to Live By
How to Fast Successfully
Shaping History through Prayer and Fasting
The Grace of Yielding
The Marriage Covenant
Chords from David's Harp

Systematic Bible Exposition:
The Foundation Series
  Book 1: Foundation for Faith
  Book 2: Repent and Believe
  Book 3: From Jordan to Pentecost
  Book 4: Purposes of Pentecost
  Book 5: Laying On of Hands
  Book 6: Resurrection of the Dead
  Book 7: Eternal Judgment
The Last Word on the Middle East
Self-Study Bible Course

Derek Prince Ministries
P.O. Box 300
Fort Lauderdale, FL 33302-0300

GOD IS A MATCH-MAKER

DEREK PRINCE
with RUTH PRINCE

Published by

FLEMING H. REVELL COMPANY
OLD TAPPAN, NEW JERSEY

Library of Congress Cataloging in Publication Data

Prince, Derek.
  God is a matchmaker.

  1. Marriage—Religious aspects—Christianity. 2. Prince, Derek. I. Title.
BV835.P75   1986   248.8'4   85-29891
ISBN 0-8007-9058-8

Designed by Ann McMath

A Chosen Book
Copyright © 1986 by **Derek Prince**
Chosen Books are Published by
Fleming H. Revell Company
Old Tappan, New Jersey
Printed in the United States of America

Contents

BACKGROUND OF THE AUTHOR

Born in India of British parents, Derek Prince was educated in the classics at two of Britain's most prestigious institutions: Eton College and Cambridge University. At an unusually early age he became a professor of philosophy at Cambridge University. Called into the British Army in World War II, he took along a Bible to study as a "work of philosophy." One night, alone in a barracks room, he was confronted with the reality of Jesus Christ, and his life's direction was totally changed.

Since then—now more than forty years—Derek Prince has served as pastor, counselor, educator and Bible teacher on four continents. He has worked extensively with young people from varied racial backgrounds. Through his personal ministry in churches and conferences, thousands in many lands have been healed and delivered from evil spirits.

Derek Prince is internationally recognized as one of the leading Bible expositors of our time. His radio program, "Today with Derek Prince," is heard on more than 60 stations in the U.S., as well as in China, India, Central and South America, the Middle East and parts of Africa, Australia, New Zealand, and the islands of the Pacific and the Caribbean. He has authored more than 20 books, most of which have been translated into several foreign languages. His hundreds of teaching messages on cassette are reaching every area of the earth, including Communist and Moslem lands.

In this book Derek Prince relates the story of his two marriages. Through his marriage to his first wife, Lydia, in Jerusalem at the end of World War II, he became father to the eight girls in her children's home there. Of these, six are Jewish, one Arab, and one English. Later, in Kenya, they adopted an African baby girl.

In 1978, three years after Lydia's death, Derek Prince married his present wife, Ruth. Her three adopted Jewish children bring their family to a total of twelve, with dozens of grandchildren and great-grandchildren. In chapters 8 and 12, Ruth tells her own story.

Today Derek and Ruth Prince have two home bases, one in Fort Lauderdale, Florida, and one in Jerusalem, Israel.

Introduction

I can best introduce this book by explaining what it is not. First of all, it is not a book of mere theory or theology. It does not deal with truth in the abstract. On the contrary, it is rooted directly and firmly in the experiences of real life—my own experiences.

For more than forty years now, this has generally been the way I have made my most important discoveries in the spiritual life. They never came to me while I was seated behind a desk, pondering abstractions. Most often they were both prompted and confirmed by situations I lived through. Only later, as I meditated on such situations in light of the Bible, did I come to discern the underlying spiritual principles God had been teaching me.

In the second and third chapters of this book, I relate the way in which God led me into marriage—first with Lydia, then with Ruth. In each case, the path by which God took me corresponded exactly with the basic biblical pattern for entering into marriage.

The first time I really did not understand what God had done. When the pattern was repeated in my second marriage, I came to realize that, in each marriage, God had followed the very same pattern He Himself had established at the dawn of human history—a pattern He has ordained to stand unchanged until human history reaches its consummation. *It is this divine pattern for entering into marriage that is the central theme of this book.*

I need to explain, too, that this book does not attempt to lay out a plan for married life or for the raising of a family. There are a number of excellent books currently available on these themes. Rather, my purpose is to explain the steps that lead up to a successful marriage. A man and a woman who seek God's direction only *after* they have exchanged vows in a church are like the man Jesus pictured who built his house on sand. All too often, such a marriage will not stand up to the tests and pressures to which it will almost inevitably be subjected.

This book will help you to answer some of the most important questions with which life confronts you: How can I know if it is God's will for me to marry? If it is God's will, how can I prepare myself for marriage? And how can I find the mate God has appointed for me?

In chapter 8, Ruth offers suggestions specifically for women on preparation for marriage. Again in the final chapter, Ruth shares very personal details of her own preparation to be my wife.

Chapter 9 offers special counsel for parents, which will help them to guide their children through that difficult and dangerous phase of life in which they wrestle with the emotional and spiritual problems of choosing a mate.

The same chapter provides constructive material for pastors, counselors, teachers, youth ministers, and all the other servants of God who seek to lead His people into lives of fulfillment and fruitfulness. There is no area where sound, biblical instruction is needed more than in the application of God's pattern for marriage to contemporary living.

Chapters 10 and 11 offer much-needed help to the many millions who are confronted with special, critical problems in this whole area of marriage: those who have passed through the agony of divorce, and those destined to live out their lives unmarried.

There is one other category of people to whom this book may appeal: those who enjoy a true-life romance with an element of suspense! Ruth and I hope you will enjoy this part of our story. And remember, the suspense will not be resolved until you reach Ruth's final chapter, "Meet Me in the King David"!

Derek Prince
Jerusalem

My School of Experience

1

The Voices of
Bride and Bridegroom

> Then the Lord God made a woman from the rib he
> had taken out of the man, and he brought her to
> the man. (Genesis 2:22)

God first appeared on the scene of human history in the
role of a matchmaker. What a profound and exciting
revelation!

Is it too much to suggest that Eve came to Adam on the
arm of the Lord Himself, in the same way that a bride today
walks down the aisle of the church on her father's arm? What
human mind can fathom the depth of love and joy that filled
the heart of the great Creator as He united the man and
woman in this first marriage ceremony?

Surely this account is one among countless indications that
the Bible is not a work of merely human authorship. Moses is
generally accepted as the author of the creation record. But
apart from supernatural inspiration, he would never have
dared to open human history with a scene of such amazing
intimacy—intimacy first between God and man, and then
between man and woman.

The portrait Moses here paints of God is in a totally different category from the type of religious art we have come to associate with churches and cathedrals. It is doubtful, in fact, if Moses' portrait would even find a place on their walls or in their windows.

Not only does human history open with a marriage. It is also destined to climax with a marriage. It is John on Patmos who paints this scene for us in Revelation 19:6–9:

> Then I heard what sounded like a great multitude, like the roar of rushing waters and like loud peals of thunder, shouting:
>
> "Hallelujah!
>   For our Lord God Almighty reigns.
> Let us rejoice and be glad
>   and give him glory!
> For the wedding of the Lamb has come,
>   and his bride has made herself ready.
> Fine linen, bright and clean,
>   was given her to wear."
> [Fine linen stands for the righteous acts of the
>   saints.]
>
> Then the angel said to me, "Write: 'Blessed are those who are invited to the wedding supper of the Lamb!' "

The spectacle that John exposes briefly to our gaze is one of triumph, of praise and worship, of feasting and splendor, of almost uncontainable joy. Most wonderful of all, it is almighty God Himself, the Creator and Ruler of the universe, who presides over this, the marriage ceremony of His own Son. As it unfolds, heaven and earth blend together in a symphony of praise and worship such as the universe has never before heard.

It is characteristic of the Bible's restraint that it makes no attempt to describe the feelings of the heavenly Bridegroom and His Bride. No human language contains the vocabulary that would be needed. This is an area of holy mystery, reserved for the Lord Himself and for those who, by diligent preparation, "have made themselves ready."

From Genesis to Revelation, from the first act in Eden to the last act in the heavenlies, the central theme of human history is marriage. Throughout this unfolding drama, God Himself does not remain merely a remote spectator. It is He who initiates the action, and it is in Him that it comes to its climax. From beginning to end, He is totally and personally involved.

When Jesus came to earth to make God known to man, His attitude toward marriage harmonized perfectly with that of the Father. Just as the Father opened human history with a marriage, so Jesus opened His public ministry at the marriage in Cana. When the wine ran out at the height of the celebration, Mary turned to Jesus for help. He responded by converting about 150 gallons of water into wine.

No ordinary wine, either! For the master of the banquet, after tasting it, called the bridegroom aside and said, "Everyone brings out the choice wine first and then the cheaper wine after the guests have had too much to drink; but you have saved the best till now" (John 2:10).

What prompted Jesus to perform His first miracle in such a setting? What important truth did He demonstrate by it? The answer is simple: He demonstrated how much He cared about the success of the wedding. Had the wine run out, the bridegroom and the bride would have been publicly humiliated, and the wedding would have ended in gloom. To forestall such a disaster, Jesus granted the first release on earth of His miracle-working power.

Furthermore, Jesus was careful to perform the miracle in

such a way that none of the guests knew what had happened. He attracted no attention to Himself. He demonstrated that in every marriage there is only one proper focus of attention: the bride and the groom. Although it was Jesus who performed the miracle, the public recognition actually went to the bridegroom.

In His subsequent public teaching ministry, Jesus consistently upheld the plan of marriage initiated at creation by the Father. For this reason, He rejected the standard of marriage current in His day. When confronted by some Pharisees with a question about divorce, He replied: "Haven't you read that at the beginning the Creator 'made them male and female,' and said, 'For this reason a man will leave his father and mother and be united to his wife, and the two will become one flesh'? So they are no longer two, but one. Therefore what God has joined together, let man not separate" (Matthew 19:4–6).

In the Hebrew Old Testament, the title of the book we call Genesis is taken from the opening words of the book, "At the beginning." By answering the Pharisees with this phrase, Jesus deliberately directed them to the book of Genesis, and in particular to the way in which God had united Eve with Adam. In other words, He upheld the plan of marriage established there by the Father as still in force in His day, and as the only divinely ordained standard for marriage. He refused to lend His authority to any lower standard.

The Pharisees countered by referring to an ordinance in the Law of Moses that permitted divorce for reasons other than marital unfaithfulness. To this Jesus replied, "Moses permitted you to divorce your wives because your hearts were hard. But it was not this way from the beginning" (Matthew 19:8). Once again Jesus directed them to the beginning—that is, to the pattern established at the opening of Genesis. It was the only pattern He accepted. Any deviation from it was not the will of the Father, but merely a concession to the hard heart of unregenerate man.

This conversation of Jesus with the Pharisees has important implications for us as Christians today. The divine standard of marriage in force for us is still that established by God at creation. Any lowering of this standard is merely a concession to the hardness of man's unregenerate heart.

Christians who have been born again of God's Spirit are a "new creation," no longer subject to the dictates of their old, unregenerate nature. For Christians today, therefore, the divine standard of marriage is that established by God at creation and upheld by Jesus throughout His ministry.

Specifically, the Genesis account reveals four vitally important truths about marriage, all of which still apply today.

First, the concept of marriage originated entirely with God. Adam had no part in it. It was not a plan he formulated. He did not even ask for such a provision. It was God, not Adam, who decided that Adam needed a wife. Adam was not aware of his own need.

Second, it was God who formed Eve for Adam. He alone knew the kind of mate Adam needed.

Third, it was God who presented Eve to Adam. Adam did not have to go in search of her.

And fourth, it was God who determined the way in which Adam and Eve were to relate to each other. The end purpose of their relationship was perfect unity: "For this reason a man will leave his father and mother and be united to his wife, and they will become one flesh" (Genesis 2:24).

If, as Jesus indicated, God's pattern for marriage remains unchanged for Christians today, then the four truths outlined above still apply in our lives. In practical terms, what does this entail?

That a Christian will enter into marriage not because it is his or her decision, but because it is God's.

That a Christian man will trust God both to choose and to prepare for him the mate he needs. On the other side, a Christian woman will trust God to prepare her for the husband for whom God has appointed her.

That a Christian man, walking in the will of God, will find that God brings to him the mate whom He has chosen and prepared for him. On the other side, a Christian woman will allow God to lead her to the husband for whom He has been preparing her.

That the end purpose of marriage today is still what it was for Adam and Eve—perfect unity. Only those who fulfill the first three requirements, however, can expect also to enjoy the fulfillment of the end purpose.

Some may be tempted to dismiss these principles as old-fashioned or "super-spiritual." There is never any devaluation of the currency of the Kingdom of God, however, no erosion of its values and standards. For those who are truly following Jesus, the requirements are just the same as they were in Jesus' own day. But—thank God—so also are the rewards!

For me, these principles are not mere abstract theories. In both of my marriages they were worked out exactly, as I shall recount in the next two chapters. In each case, the decision to marry originated with God, not with me. Indeed, I myself was not seeking marriage. In each case, God chose my wife for me, prepared her for me, and brought her to me. Most important of all, each of my marriages has produced a degree of unity that few couples today enjoy.

All this did not result from my following some elaborate theological theory as to how a man should enter into marriage. Rather, it was brought about by the sovereign guidance and overruling of the Holy Spirit in my life. Many times I was not even conscious that it was the Holy Spirit who was at work. Gradually, however, as I pondered on the course of my life in the light of Scripture, I came to see, in each of my marriages, how God had worked exactly according to the pattern that He Himself had established "at the beginning." I share these principles now because I know they work. I can wish for my fellow believers no greater happiness than they have brought to me.

This brief analysis of the biblical pattern of marriage stands in sharp contrast with the standards of the world today—or even with those accepted in many sections of the Church. The prevailing attitude toward marriage in any culture or civilization is usually an accurate barometer revealing its moral and spiritual climate. The decline of a culture is marked by a decline in its respect for marriage. Conversely, the renewal of a culture is marked by a corresponding renewal of the biblical values of marriage.

There are various passages in the Bible that depict how marriage is affected by both a period of decline and a period of restoration. In Jeremiah 25:10–11, God warns the people of Judah of the desolation to be brought upon them by Nebuchadnezzar's impending invasion: "I will banish from them the sounds of joy and gladness, the voices of bride and bridegroom, the sound of millstones and the light of the lamp. This whole country will become a desolate wasteland. . . ."

The apostle John paints a similar picture of the end-time destruction of the anti-Christian system known as "Great Babylon":

> The music of harpists and musicians, flute players
> and trumpeters,
> will never be heard in you again.
> No workman of any trade
> will ever be found in you again.
> The sound of a millstone
> will never be heard in you again.

The light of a lamp
    will never shine in you again.
The voice of bridegroom and bride
    will never be heard in you again.
                            (Revelation 18:22–23)

One conspicuous feature central to both these descriptions of decline and desolation is the silencing of the voices of bridegroom and bride. A culture that no longer makes the joyful celebration of marriage central to its way of life is either doomed already or on its way to doom.

The converse is equally true. Restoration of a culture will be marked by restoration of marriage as a source of joy and a cause for celebration. In Jeremiah 33:10–11 God promises the end-time restoration of Judah and Israel:

> This is what the Lord says: "You say about this place, 'It is a desolate waste, without men or animals.' Yet in the towns of Judah and the streets of Jerusalem that are deserted, inhabited by neither men nor animals, there will be heard once more the sounds of joy and gladness, the voices of bride and bridegroom, and the voices of those who bring thank offerings to the house of the Lord. . . . For I will restore the fortunes of the land as they were before," says the Lord.

Once again in this picture—as in desolation, so in restoration—bride and groom are central. By the standards of Scripture, the restoration of a people is incomplete unless heralded by "the voices of bride and bridegroom."

Various forces may undermine the biblical foundations of marriage. Secular humanism, for example, presents marriage as a kind of social contract in which the parties are free to dictate their own terms and conditions, and to modify or abrogate them at will if their feelings change. People who approach marriage on this basis will never experience either the physical or the spiritual fulfillment that the Bible promises to those who follow its pattern.

On the other side, however, formal religion without the grace of God can have an almost equally harmful effect on marriage. Both romance and passion are integral parts of marriage, as revealed in the Bible. Each is depicted vividly and beautifully in the Song of Songs. A marriage that lacks these is, by biblical standards, sadly incomplete. Romance without passion ends in frustration. Passion without romance is little more than lust, thinly veiled.

Over the centuries the Church has often failed to present the Bible's picture of total marriage, embracing every area of the human personality—spiritual, emotional and physical. Sex has been treated as an unfortunate necessity, almost an aberration of the Creator, which requires some kind of apology. Certainly that is not the Creator's own view. He created man and woman sexual beings, and then, after careful inspection, pronounced everything "very good"—including their sexuality.

Today, around the earth, God is visiting and renewing His Church by the Holy Spirit. This renewal must be heralded, as divine renewal has always been, by "the voices of bride and bridegroom." The Church cannot experience a full or valid renewal unless it once again embraces the biblical pattern of marriage. This must include not only the marriage ceremony and the life that follows. It must begin where marriage always begins—with the steps leading up to the ceremony.

This principle applies to almost all forms of human activity. The process of preparation is usually an essential factor in a successful outcome. A couple who decide to build a house, for instance, must go through months of preparation before they receive the key and walk through the front door. They must choose a site, hire an architect and a contractor, discuss plans of many kinds, and make countless decisions concerning all the details of style and decoration. A couple who take no interest in their home until the day they receive the key are doomed to fearful frustrations and disappointments after they begin to live in it.

If this is true of a house built of brick or stone or timber, how much more does it apply to a house built of living stones—human beings, creatures of measureless complexity but also of measureless potential?

No, a successful marriage does not begin with the wedding ceremony. Its foundation is laid much earlier—first, in the careful preparation of character, and then in the matching of a man and woman whom God has appointed for one another.

A couple entering marriage unprepared and ill-matched are doomed at best to endless frustration, and, more often than not, to total failure. On the other hand, a Christian man and woman who have allowed the Holy Spirit to mold them and lead them along the biblical path that leads to the wedding ceremony can look forward with confidence to a married life of fulfillment and mutual delight.

2

Lydia

At the very beginning of human history God established a principle: "It is not good for the man to be alone. I will make a helper suitable for him" (Genesis 2:18).

No man is complete by himself. Every man needs companionship. To meet this need, God ordained marriage and provided Adam with a wife. Marriage is the closest and most intimate form of companionship possible between two people. It is so close, in fact, that the two actually become one.

In Ephesians 5 Paul calls marriage a "mystery." In the Song of Songs Solomon compares it to a "locked garden." No academic discipline, such as psychology or theology, can unfold the mystery or open up the locked garden. God alone holds the key. He places it in the hands of those who follow Him in the path of faith and obedience.

An unmarried person may enjoy the best of counseling; he may read all the most recommended books; he may mingle freely with married couples; he may indulge in sex outside of marriage. But he still remains on the outside—uninitiated.

There is an element in marriage that cannot be explained. It can only be experienced.

For this reason, I would like to share in a very personal way the story of my marriage to Lydia. God led me, sovereignly and supernaturally, to the mate of His choice, and in so doing placed in my hand the key that opened up the mystery. Someone has said that the best school in the world is the school of experience—but it is also the most expensive!

By 1940, after many years of study, I was securely established as a professor of philosophy at Cambridge University. Then, ruthlessly, I was uprooted from my academic background and plunged into the maelstrom of World War II. Drafted into the British Army as a hospital attendant, I brought with me a Bible, which I proposed to study "as a work of philosophy." I completely discounted any theories of divine inspiration.

One night about nine months later, in an Army barrack room, I received a direct, personal revelation of Jesus Christ. The next week, in the same room, I experienced what I knew must be a supernatural infilling of the Holy Spirit. Before I had time to analyze what was taking place, I heard the syllables of some strange language proceeding from my lips. It sounded Oriental—something like Chinese or Japanese.

Although I had no idea what I was saying, I knew somehow I was communicating directly with God. Inwardly I had a marvelous sense of release from fears and tensions I had not even realized were there. And suddenly I knew I had crossed the threshold of an entirely new world.

The following night as I lay on my straw mattress—the Army's apology for a bed—I began to speak once more the strange sounds of an unknown language. This time I was struck by their rhythm, which sounded poetic. After they ceased, there was a brief pause, and then I began to speak English once more. But I was not choosing the words I was speaking, which I noticed repeated the rhythm of the words of the unknown language. I seemed to be speaking *to* myself, in the second person, but the words did not originate with me. With a sense of awe, I realized that God was using my own lips to speak to me.

In beautiful, poetic language, the Lord painted a picture of what lay ahead of me in His purposes. The picture contained scenes and images that could never have proceeded out of my own imagination. Nor could my memory retain them all. What did remain, however, indelibly engraved on my mind, was this: "It shall be like a little stream. The little stream shall become a river; the river shall become a great river; the great river shall become a sea; and the sea shall become a mighty ocean. . . ." Somehow I knew those words contained the key to God's purpose for my life.

In the ensuing days, as I meditated on these experiences and wondered what lay ahead, a name was imprinted strongly on my mind. It was *Palestine,* then the name for the area in the Middle East presently divided between Israel and Jordan. I did not understand all God was saying about His plan for my life, but I had a strong, continuing impression that it was linked somehow with the land and the people of Palestine.

A few weeks later, my unit was sent overseas to the Middle East. I had speculated that our destination might prove to be Palestine. But instead I spent the next three years in the deserts of Egypt, Libya, and the Sudan. I found myself surrounded by barrenness, both natural and spiritual. My one unfailing source of strength was my Bible, which I read through several times. But in spite of the barrenness all around, I felt that God was beginning to work out His plan for my life, and that it would be associated in some way with Palestine.

In the Sudan I met a fellow Christian soldier who had spent some time in Palestine. As we shared together, he said: "If you want a real spiritual blessing, there's a little children's home in Palestine, just north of Jerusalem, that you need to visit. It's run by a Danish lady. Soldiers are going there from all over the Middle East, and God is meeting them in a wonderful way."

I found it strange that soldiers should have to go to a children's home to be blessed, but I made a mental note of his information. The mention of Palestine stirred something in me. Also, I was weary of deserts and yearned for a change of scenery.

Then one day, quite unexpectedly, I received word that I was being transferred to Palestine. A month later I found myself in a small medical supply depot located at Kiriat Motzkin, just north of Haifa. My responsibilities were minimal and left me plenty of time for prayer.

At the first opportunity I paid a visit to the children's home, and I quickly understood why soldiers were making their way there from so many places. The atmosphere was permeated by an invisible presence that settled like dew on men weary from the strain and monotony of desert warfare. I felt my own spirit being washed from the dust of three years in barren deserts.

The woman in charge introduced herself as Lydia Christensen and gave me a warm welcome. She was a typical Scandinavian—blonde and blue-eyed. Over a cup of coffee, she related briefly how she had come to Jerusalem from Denmark sixteen years before and had begun by taking one dying Jewish baby in a basement room.* From that humble beginning, a large "family" had grown up with children from various racial backgrounds.

"I never went looking for children," Lydia told me. "I only took those I knew the Lord had sent to me."

---

*Lydia has told her story in *Appointment in Jerusalem*, (1975), published by Chosen/Zondervan.

In response, I began to share with her how the Lord had revealed Himself to me in a barrack room and had filled me with the Holy Spirit. Then I described the three years that had followed in the desert, with my Bible as my only source of strength and guidance.

"I'm not fully clear as to what the future holds," I concluded, "but I feel that God has a plan for my life, and that it has something to do with Palestine."

Lydia suggested that we should pray about it, which is what I had been longing for, and I concurred immediately. To my surprise, however, Lydia summoned some of the little girls to join us in prayer. Four or five of them trooped quickly into the room and took their seats. Lydia spoke a few words in Arabic—explaining, I assumed, what we were to pray about. Then each girl knelt in front of her chair. Lydia and I knelt, too.

As we began to pray, I sensed I was keeping an appointment with God. At one point, I heard one little girl beside me singing in clear, melodic tones. At first I thought the words were Arabic; then I realized it was another language. After a little while, the other girls joined her, also in other languages. I felt my spirit being lifted on this volume of supernatural worship to a new level of communion with the Lord. Though I did not understand what was being prayed, I knew that my entire future had been placed securely into the hands of God.

Back at the medical depot, I found my thoughts returning often to the little home in Ramallah. At the back of my mind, I could still hear the children's clear voices lifted in worship. I decided to pray regularly for Lydia. In the few hours I had spent in the home, I had perceived how many burdens she had to bear, with no helper except one Arab maid. Besides, where did she get the money to feed and clothe all those children? She had mentioned that she was not sent out by any missionary organization.

One day, alone among the long rows of bales containing medical supplies, I felt a special urge to pray for Lydia. I prayed for a while in English; then the Holy Spirit took over and gave me a clear, forceful utterance in, again, an unknown tongue. After a brief pause, an interpretation followed in English. Once again, as on that first night, it was God speaking to me through my own lips, saying: "I have joined you together . . . under the same yoke and in the same harness. . . ."

More followed, but those were the words that gripped me. What did they mean? Since it was Lydia I had been praying for, they must refer to her. Had God joined the two of us together? If so, in what way—and for what purpose?

Some months later, the Army transferred me once more— this time to a full-scale hospital in the Augusta Victoria Hospice on the Mount of Olives, east of Jerusalem. From here it was an easy journey by bus to Ramallah. My visits to the children's home became frequent, and my fellowship there deepened, with both Lydia and the children.

My time for discharge from the Army was now less than a year away. I became more and more convinced that God was directing me to obtain my discharge in Palestine and then stay on there in full-time service for Him. But what kind of service—and with whom?

There were two active Full Gospel churches in Jerusalem. I had become friendly with the leaders of each. Should I offer my services to one of them? Then, of course, there was the children's home in Ramallah. That was where I enjoyed the closest fellowship. But what part would I play in a children's home?

Besides, there was the question of my financial support. In Britain, before I met the Lord, I had not even been a churchgoer, must less a minister. I was unknown to Christians there. What motive would they have for supporting me?

I had a Christian friend named Geoffrey working with a medical unit in Jerusalem, whose help I solicited in prayer. I knew Geoffrey to be sensitive to the Lord's voice. Also, he was familiar with the two Full Gospel churches as well as the children's home. "I need to know which of them the Lord wants me to commit myself to," I told him.

Geoffrey himself was working closely with one of the Full Gospel churches and obviously felt that would be the place for me, too. He was ready to pray with me, however, and after praying for each of the Full Gospel churches, he began to pray for Lydia and the children's home.

"Lord," he said, "You have shown me that that little home will be like a little stream, and the little stream will become a river, and the river will become a great river, and the great river will become a sea. . . ."

I did not hear another word Geoffrey prayed! I was overwhelmed with excitement, and yet with awe. Geoffrey had repeated word for word exactly what God had said to me about my future that night in the barrack room in Britain, but he had applied the words to Lydia and the children's home. In the years in between, I had never shared those words with another soul. Only God could have given them to Geoffrey.

"Thank you," I said to Geoffrey when he had finished praying. "I believe I know what God wants me to do." But I never told him how I knew!

I had much to ponder. Back in Britain, God had spoken about my future and given me the picture of a little stream continually being enlarged. Then, in the depot in Kiriat Motzkin as I was praying for Lydia, God had said He had "joined us together under the same yoke and in the same harness." Now I discovered that God had given Geoffrey— concerning Lydia and the children's home—exactly the same picture of an enlarging stream that He had given me.

I was reminded of the two related expressions God had

used in Kiriat Motzkin: *Under the same yoke and in the same harness.* A harness pictured two animals working together in close relationship. But what about a yoke? I suddenly realized that this was a picture used regularly in the Bible of two persons united in marriage. Could that be what God had in mind?

I began to dwell on the differences and the difficulties. Lydia was from a cultural background quite unlike mine. She was a strong character, a natural leader. In the face of endless difficulties, she had built a work that had earned her the respect of the Christian community. She was used to fighting her own battles. Would she be willing to surrender headship in the home to a man much younger and less experienced than herself? Would it even be practical for her to do so?

Then there was the difference in our ages. I was in my early thirties, while Lydia, an amazingly vital and active person, was in middle age. A marriage between two persons so different in age would inevitably face unusual pressures.

I had my own background to consider, too. I was an only child. My educational background was totally intellectual. Though I could build philosophical theories about humanity, I knew very little about dealing with real human beings. Could I become father to a family of girls—girls whose racial and cultural backgrounds were totally alien to mine? Would it even be fair to impose such a father on those girls?

All that was on the negative side. The positive side could be summed up in one brief sentence: *God had spoken.* Clearly, supernaturally, He had revealed His plan—first of all to me alone. Then, through a fellow Christian, He had confirmed it just as clearly, just as supernaturally. This had not come in response to my prayers, or even my desires. The whole revelation had its source solely in the sovereign will of God. If I were to reject God's will so clearly revealed, how could I expect His blessing on my future?

I was torn between excitement and fear: excitement at the thought that God had such a clearly marked-out plan for my life; fear that the task ahead would prove too difficult. Eventually I realized that I could not reason it all out in advance. That was not what God was asking of me. He was asking me to commit myself in faith to the plan He had revealed, and then to allow Him to work out for me the things I could not work out for myself.

Finally I came to this point of commitment. So far as I understood God's plan for my life, I embraced it. What I did not yet understand, I would trust God to reveal in His own way and time.

From this point onward, there was a progressive change in my relationship with Lydia. Our fellowship was already close and enriching to us both. But now it took on a new warmth and intimacy, which increased each time I visited the home. For the children, too, I began to feel a kind of parental concern I had never known before. Eventually I had to acknowledge it to myself: I was in love—in love with Lydia and in love with the eight children.

A few months later, it seemed altogether natural for me to ask Lydia to marry me, and just as natural for her to say yes. Early in 1946 we were married, about a month before the Army granted me my discharge.

Later that year we moved the home from Ramallah to Jerusalem, where we were caught up in the tumultuous train of events that proved to be the labor pains of the birth of the State of Israel. Our lives were frequently in danger. We had to move house four times—twice at night. War and famine were all around us. Yet God protected and provided for us in ways that continually amazed us. Sharing all these experiences as a family knit us together with bonds closer than those of many natural families—bonds that still hold today.

From Jerusalem we moved to London, where I pastored a

congregation for eight years. By the end of this period, the older girls had grown up and left home, all but one of them married. With the two youngest girls, Lydia and I moved to Kenya, where I served for five years as principal of a Teacher Training College for Africans. From Kenya the two remaining girls left us, to pursue careers and then marriage. It was here, too, that we adopted Jesika, a six-month-old African baby girl, who became our ninth daughter.

In 1962 Lydia and Jesika and I moved to North America, first to Canada and then to the United States, where we finally settled. Here God opened doors of ministry to us in every part of the nation, and then in many other nations.

The family was increasing steadily in numbers, meanwhile, and had spread abroad to various parts of the earth, with members settled in Britain, Canada, the United States, and Australia. "The sun never sets on our family," Lydia sometimes commented. The little stream that started in Ramallah was becoming a river that encircled the globe.

Throughout these years, Lydia and I had one main source of strength that never failed us: our unity. In our personal prayer life we were continually enabled to claim the promise of Matthew 18:19: "Again, I tell you that if two of you on earth agree about anything you ask for, it will be done for you by my Father in heaven." There is no way to count the specific prayers that we saw answered on this basis.

In our public ministry, too, as we prayed for long hours with the sick and afflicted, our unity brought us victories that neither of us could ever have gained alone. A fellow minister once commented, "You two work together just like one person."

In 1975, after almost thirty years, God called Lydia home. She had given Him more than fifty years of arduous, selfless service. A fitting tribute to her is found in Proverbs 31:28–29:

> Her children arise and call her blessed;
>   her husband also, and he praises her:
> Many women do noble things,
>   but you surpass them all.

The more I meditate on my marriage with Lydia, the more I marvel at God's flawless wisdom. At the time we were married, I had no inkling of the kind of life that lay ahead of us. So I had no basis for choosing a wife for myself, since I lacked the essential information on which alone an intelligent choice could be based. Looking back over the labors and trials and battles of thirty years, on the other hand, I am convinced that Lydia was the only woman in the world who could have been a sufficient helper for me through it all.

How wonderful, then, that God knew just the kind of wife I would need; that for many years He prepared her for me; that He placed her in the path by which He purposed to lead me; and that He pointed her out to me as the helper He had chosen for me. Each time I go over this in my mind, I bow my head in worship and say with Paul:

> Oh, the depth of the riches of the wisdom and
>   knowledge of God!
> How unsearchable his judgments,
>   and his paths beyond tracing out!

(Romans 11:33)

3

Ruth

After Lydia's death, I experienced a sense of loneliness such as I had never even imagined. Bereavement is something almost all of us have to face at some time. Yet so few people, even among committed Christians, are really prepared for it. Through it, I learned in a new measure my need of the Body of Christ.

Over the years I had been drawn into a close relationship with four other nationally known Bible teachers: Don Basham, Ern Baxter, Bob Mumford, and Charles Simpson. We had committed ourselves to share together in prayer, in counsel, and in fellowship. In this way we sought to uphold and strengthen one another.

The comfort I received from my brothers in those hours of loneliness helped to turn sorrow into ultimate joy and victory. The day came when I could say with David: "Thou hast turned for me my mourning into dancing: thou hast put off my sackcloth, and girded me with gladness . . ." (Psalm 30:11 KJV).

In the summer of 1977, the five of us were part of a group

of international charismatic leaders, both Catholic and Protestant, who made a pilgrimage to the Holy Land. In Jerusalem we had the privilege of joining with Cardinal Suenens of Belgium in celebrating his fiftieth year in the priesthood. When the rest of the group left, I decided to stay on in Israel for one more week. I set these days aside to seek the Lord as to whether the time had come for me to turn my face again toward Jerusalem. I knew my ministry there was not yet complete.

I also took the opportunity to visit the office of an organization that had been active in translating and circulating my books in Israel and elsewhere. While there, I recalled a letter I had received from them some time previously ending with a handwritten postscript: "I want to thank you for your ministry. It has meant much to me over the years. Ruth Baker."

I felt I should take this opportunity to express my appreciation, but the receptionist at the office told me Ruth Baker had seriously injured her back two months previously and was at home in her apartment, unable to work.

Over the years God had given me a special gift of faith to minister to people with back problems. Most of those I prayed for were healed—some immediately, some gradually. I certainly had not come to Jerusalem to visit the sick, but felt it would be ungracious on my part if I did not at least offer my help.

"Do you think the lady would like me to pray for her?" I inquired at the office. The staff responded with a unanimous and enthusiastic yes, and gave directions to her apartment.

A young man named David had put a car at my disposal and was driving me around Jerusalem, so we set out for the address we had been given. After we had driven for forty minutes without success up and down Jerusalem's narrow, inadequately marked streets, I said to David, "We must be out of the Lord's will. Let's turn around and head for home."

At the very point where David began to turn the car, I looked once more at the number on the house across the street. It was the building we had been looking for!

We found the lady lying on a divan in her living room. I saw on her face the strained look of pain so common to people with back injuries. After giving her some instruction on how to release her faith, I laid my hand on her head and began to pray. Then, unexpectedly, the Lord gave me a prophetic word for her that contained both encouragement and direction. From the light it brought to her features, I could tell it had spoken to her inner needs. We talked a few minutes, and then I took my leave with a sense of duty done.

I went out very little for the rest of the week, concentrating on seeking an answer from God concerning my future. But no answer came. My last day in Israel arrived, and still I had heard nothing from God. I was due to leave early the next morning from Ben Gurion Airport.

That night I went to bed about 11 p.m., but did not sleep. Suddenly I realized that the barriers were down and I was in direct contact with God. I had no further thought of sleep. For the rest of the night God spoke to me. For the most part, I heard His voice speaking within my spirit with a quiet authority that could come from no other source but God Himself.

He reminded me of the course that my life had taken up to that time. Many instances and circumstances passed before my mind, in which God had intervened on my behalf to protect and guide me. He reminded me, too, of the various promises He had given me over the years—those that had already been fulfilled and those that had yet to be fulfilled. He assured me that if I would continue to walk in obedience, all of them would find fulfillment.

Then, in the early hours of the morning, a strange but vivid picture appeared before my eyes. I saw a hill sloping steeply upward before me, a hill that reminded me of the one sloping up to Mount Zion at the southwest corner of the Old City of Jerusalem. A zig-zag path wound its way up the hill from its base to its summit.

Instinctively I knew that this represented the path back to Jerusalem for me. It would climb steeply uphill all the way. There would be many sharp turns in it, first one way and then the other. But if I set my face and persevered, it would take me to the place God had appointed for me in Jerusalem.

The most striking feature in the picture I saw before me was the figure of a woman seated on the ground just at the point where the path started up the hill. Her features were European, her coloring blonde. But she was wearing what looked to be an Oriental-style dress, in a color hard to define but predominantly green. What particularly struck me was her unusual posture. Her back was bent forward in a strained, unnatural position, suggesting pain. Suddenly I recognized her. It was Ruth Baker.

Why had God brought this woman before me, and in such a strange context? Before I had even formulated the question, I knew the answer. It did not come to me through any process of reasoning. It was not even something God spoke to me. It was just there, settled in an area of my mind to which doubt had no access. *God intended the woman to become my wife.*

I knew with equal certainty why the woman was seated just at the point where the path started upward. There was no other way of access to the path. Marrying her would be the first step in my way back to Israel. God had left me no options.

A whole succession of emotions flooded my inner being— amazement, fear, excitement. For a moment I was even tempted to be angry with God. How could He confront me with such a situation? Was He really asking me to marry a woman I had met only once, one I knew nothing about? I waited to see if God had something more to say about this—some explanation, perhaps. But nothing more came.

I saw that I needed to act with great caution. I was a well-known figure in certain Christian circles. If I were to make a foolish move now, especially in the area of marriage, I would bring dishonor to the Lord and become a stumblingblock to His people. I decided not to tell anyone about what had happened. I would simply hold the matter before the Lord in prayer and seek further direction from Him.

For a month, once back in the States, I prayed—earnestly, continually. Nothing changed. The vision did not fade from my mind. If anything, it became more vivid. At the end of the month, I still felt God had left me no options. He intended me to marry Ruth Baker.

Eventually I said to myself, "Faith without works is dead. If I really believe God has shown me His will, I had better begin to act." So I sat down and wrote a brief letter to Ruth Baker in Jerusalem, suggesting that if she ever came back to the States, she might be interested to visit a Christian fellowship in Kansas City. The people there had a special love for Israel and also close personal ties with me.

Almost by return mail I received a reply. Ruth was on the point of leaving Israel with her daughter for a visit to the United States. She was grateful for my concern and would indeed like to visit the fellowship in Kansas City. She gave some dates that would fit in with her itinerary and a phone number at which she could be reached in Maryland.

I phoned her promptly and fixed the dates for her visit to Kansas City. I myself was due to leave shortly for ministry in South Africa, but I arranged to be in Kansas City for the first two days Ruth was to be there, and to leave from there directly for South Africa.

The leader of the fellowship in Kansas City was David, the young man who had driven me around Jerusalem. He accommodated Ruth and her daughter and me in his spacious home. The second day Ruth arranged to have a counseling session with me concerning a problem that had arisen in Jerusalem.

When she came in, I complimented her on the unusual dress she was wearing. "It's Arab style," she replied. "I bought it in the Old City."

Then she went on to explain that the injury in her back made it painful for her to sit any length of time in a normal chair. With my consent, she seated herself on the floor, with her back propped against the wall and her knees turned to one side.

Unbidden, my mind went back to the woman I had seen that night sitting at the foot of the path up the hillside. Not only was it the same woman now in front of me; it was the same dress of unusual style and color, and she was seated in precisely the same strained posture that was a silent testimony of pain. Every detail was exact!

I was unable to speak. I could only stare at her in awe. Then a warm current of supernatural power surged through my body and I was filled with an inexpressible love for this woman, who was still outwardly a stranger. For a few brief moments we sat there in silence. Then, with an effort of my will, I mastered my emotions and began to inquire about the problems that had caused her to seek my counsel.

For the rest of our conversation, my mind was working on two levels simultaneously. On the one, I offered my counsel concerning Ruth's problem. On the other, I tried to take in the full implications of what was happening inside me.

Before leaving for South Africa the next day, I asked Ruth briefly about her future. She was planning to be back in Jerusalem for the Jewish New Year and Yom Kippur (the Day of Atonement), which fell that year near the end of September. Coincidentally, I had already made arrangements to return from South Africa by way of Israel and stop off for a few days in Jerusalem. I had felt an urge to be there for Yom Kippur.

All through my period of ministry in South Africa, I wondered what to do next about Ruth. Two things were now clear: that God intended me to marry her, and that I was in love with her. It was up to me to make the next move. I decided to send Ruth a telegram asking her to meet me for breakfast at 9 a.m. in the King David Hotel in Jerusalem the day before Yom Kippur.

My ministry in South Africa closed with a weekend at a church in Pretoria, where I received a generous love gift in South African rand. Currency regulations did not permit me to take the money out of the country. To change it into dollars would be a time-consuming process. Then I remembered that South Africa was famous for its diamonds. On the spur of the moment I decided to buy one.

I was directed to a jewelry store in Pretoria owned by a member of the church. He showed me a whole range of diamonds, explaining the special features of each. Finally I selected one that seemed to sparkle at me just a shade more brilliantly than the rest. The storekeeper wrapped it carefully in a piece of paper folded several times, and told me to carry it in my pocket. That seemed a casual way to carry a diamond, but I followed his instructions.

As I was about to leave the store, I noticed a beautiful double tiger's eye brooch, set in gold. The storekeeper gave me the price and I counted the rand I had left. They were just enough, so I bought the brooch as well, and had it gift-wrapped.

Two days later, at 8:45 a.m., I took my place in the lobby of the King David Hotel in Jerusalem. I chose a seat facing the revolving entrance door. One question filled my mind: Would Ruth keep the appointment?

Precisely at nine o'clock she walked through the revolving door. I rose and greeted her, then led the way to the large dining room, where an elaborate breakfast was laid out on the buffet.

To my surprise, our conversation flowed freely from the start. I described the various meetings I had held in South Africa. Then I put my hand into my pocket and pulled out the tiger's eye brooch in its gift wrapping. "I've brought you a souvenir from South Africa," I said.

Ruth opened the parcel and took out the brooch. "It's beautiful!" she exclaimed. "I really don't know how to thank you." Her eyes sparkled and a faint suspicion of a blush colored her cheeks. I was reminded of the jewel that Isaac sent to Rebecca by Abraham's servant—and all that followed when she accepted it.

After breakfast we went to the main synagogue on King George Avenue to obtain tickets for the Yom Kippur services. When we got back to the hotel, I suggested we spend the rest of the morning in deck chairs by the swimming pool, and asked Ruth to tell me about herself and the whole chain of circumstances that had brought her to Jerusalem. As I expected, a thread of suffering ran through her story, climaxing in the mercy and grace of God, who had brought her to Himself and called her to serve Him in Israel.

I was particularly interested in the answer to one question: How had her marriage ended? If by divorce, as I suspected, on what grounds? Earlier in my ministry, I had made a careful study of the Bible's teaching on divorce and remarriage. I had concluded that a person who divorces a spouse on grounds of proven unfaithfulness has a clear, biblical right to remarry, without any stigma of guilt or inferiority. Now, as I listened to Ruth's story, I was satisfied that her case fell into this category.

It seemed natural to continue our conversation at a late

lunch. But as I might have expected, Ruth's strength eventually gave out. She could talk no more. My turn had come!

After a moment's hesitation, I told her as plainly as I could about the vision I had seen of the path up the hillside, with her seated at the foot.

"That's why I invited you to meet me in Kansas City," I continued, "and why I've invited you here today. I believe it's God's purpose for us to be married and to serve Him together." Then after a pause I added, "But you can't decide on the basis of a revelation God gave me. You have to hear from Him for yourself."

Quietly and simply, Ruth replied that God had already been dealing with her about the same issue. "After we had been together in Kansas City," she said, "I told the Lord that if you were to ask me to marry you, I would say yes."

At that moment we both knew our commitment to one another had been made.

After the service in the synagogue that evening, I told Ruth about my relationship with the other four teachers.

"We've agreed not to make major personal decisions without consulting one another," I explained. "For that reason I'm not free to go any further with my commitment to you until I've spoken to my brothers. However, I believe God has made His will plain and He will work it out."

During the day of fasting that followed, Ruth and I spent much time together, waiting on God and recommitting our lives to Him for His purposes. The closer we drew to the Lord, the closer we felt also to each other.

Early the next morning I left Jerusalem. In the airplane I had time to reflect on all that had happened. How wonderful, I thought to myself, that God would arrange for us to establish our relationship with each other on the most holy day in the Jewish calendar, and to seal it with prayer and fasting!

Shortly after returning to the United States, I shared this new development in my life with Charles Simpson, although more than a month passed before I could meet together with all four of my fellow teachers. We spent half-a-day together discussing the issue of my marrying Ruth. As I told the story of how God had led me, I realized how much of it was subjective and supernatural. To me it was all so real and vivid. To others it could easily appear farfetched and fanciful.

There were other problems, too. In the breakup of her marriage, Ruth had been—as I saw it—sinned against, not sinning. Nevertheless, in Christian circles the word *divorcee* nearly always produces a negative reaction that does not necessarily take into account the finer points of biblical interpretation. For me, a prominent Bible teacher, to marry a divorced woman was bound to offend some people.

Then again, Ruth was a semi-invalid. As such, she would inevitably be more of a burden than a blessing in my active style of ministry. Personally, I was convinced Ruth's healing was already in progress. But I had to admit there was not much visible evidence to confirm this.

My brothers, naturally, were more concerned about me than about Ruth. They feared that an unsuitable marriage at this stage could compromise my whole ministry and frustrate God's purpose for the rest of my life. After lengthy discussion, they told me they simply could not endorse my marrying Ruth at that time. At my request, they gave me a letter, signed by all of them, which briefly, but graciously, explained their point of view.

At this stage I found myself faced with some of the hardest decisions of my life. My relationship with my fellow teachers was in no sense a legal contract, nor was it denominational in structure. Any one of us was free to withdraw at any time he deemed it right. Should I avail myself of that option?

In weighing this, I was not concerned so much with what

my brothers might say as with what God Himself would say. To me, there is nothing more important in life than God's favor.

I recalled David's picture in Psalm 15 of the man who finds favor with God, particularly the statement that such a man "keeps his oath even when it hurts" (verse 4). A commitment on which a person can renege when it no longer suits him is no commitment at all. Besides, in my hour of bereavement I had accepted all the support my brothers gave me. Could I accept their comfort when it suited me, and reject their counsel when it went against my own wishes?

Nothing changed in my feelings about Ruth. I was still convinced she was God's precious gift to me. Could God be asking me to release her? I remembered how God gave Isaac to Abraham, then asked for him back as a sacrifice on Mount Moriah. Only after Abraham had proved he was willing to make the sacrifice did God release His full blessing upon both Abraham, the sacrificer, and upon Isaac, the sacrifice.

I had once written a book on this theme entitled *The Grace of Yielding.* * If I myself was not willing to follow its teaching, I would be condemned in my own heart as one who preached to others what he was not prepared to practice himself. I saw that my convictions left me with no option. I must bow to my brothers' decision and communicate it to Ruth.

With a heavy heart, I phoned Ruth to tell her. The only comfort I could offer was that I would be coming out to Jerusalem in about two weeks, as I had to meet with some leaders there in connection with a tour we were planning. I promised to explain things more fully to her in person.

Two weeks later we met again for breakfast in the King David Hotel. On the surface, our meeting was surprisingly

---

*Published by Derek Prince Ministries, Fort Lauderdale, Florida (1977).

unemotional. I told Ruth all that had transpired, and handed her the letter from my brothers.

"I feel we need to break off all contact with one another," I said, "except the contact we can have by prayer."

Ruth assured me that she understood my decision and was in agreement with it. We did not need any words to affirm to each other that our feelings had not changed. Breakfast ended, I put Ruth into a taxi and followed it with my eyes until it was lost in the stream of traffic.

In the days that followed, bleak winter settled over my soul. Life was so empty. Every task was a drudgery. My closest friends seemed far from me.

Then, unexpectedly, some words formed in my mind and lingered there: *What dies in the fall will be resurrected in the spring.* I did not fully understand, yet they kindled a fresh spark of hope in my soul.

Toward the end of the year I was on my way to Australia for ministry. In the plane high over the Pacific, my eyes fell on a verse in the Bible open on my knees: "From the end of the earth will I cry unto thee, when my heart is overwhelmed: lead me to the rock that is higher than I" (Psalm 61:2, KJV). I was especially impressed since, measured from Israel, Australia is in the farthest inhabited area of the earth.

The end of the earth, I mused. *That's just where I'm going!* I read the words once more: "From the end of the earth will I cry unto thee. . . ." Was that why God was taking me to Australia? Not so much to minister to others, as to seek God in prayer for myself?

During the weeks that followed in Australia, prayer took on a new dimension for me. I fulfilled all my commitments for ministry, but kept the rest of my time for prayer. The climax came during a week in Adelaide, when I was required to minister only in the evenings. Each day, shut off in a little air-conditioned guest room at one end of a pastor's manse, I gave my whole being to prayer. Much of the time I spent on my face before God.

I had the impression that I was forcing my way through a long, dark tunnel. A place of release and fulfillment was prepared for me at the far end, but there was no way to get there except through the tunnel. My progress could be measured by the hours I spent in prayer. Finally, on the last day of the week, there was a tremendous release. I sensed I had come out into the light at the end of the tunnel.

From that moment, I knew my future with Ruth was assured. There was no more struggling, no more fretting. In the spiritual realm, the issue was settled. I could wait with quiet confidence for its outworking in the natural realm.

In the months that followed, I felt I was watching a living chessboard, on which a master hand moved one piece after the other into place. I have left it to Ruth to relate this part of our story from her perspective, which she does at the end of the book. Suffice it to say that God worked as powerfully in the hearts of my fellow teachers as He did in mine. He also granted to Ruth the perfect healing we had been trusting Him for.

In April 1978 Ruth and I announced our engagement, and in October we were married. Charles Simpson performed the ceremony and was joined by the other teachers in committing us to the Lord. How strongly we sensed God's favor upon us!

With Ruth at my side, my ministry entered a new phase. At age 63, I could easily have anticipated a gradual decline in my energy and outreach. To the contrary, however, my whole ministry expanded in ways I had never anticipated. Within a few years—through radio, books, cassettes, and personal ministry—I was reaching out to most of the globe. Most exciting of all, my radio program was touching millions who would never hear God's Word in any other way.

Ruth's unfailing love and total commitment have given me

strength and confidence to accept the new challenges God continually puts before me. But the foundation of our success has been in our ministry of daily intercession. In this we have achieved that completeness of "agreement"—of harmony in the spirit—that renders prayer undefeatable.

As Ruth and I worked side by side, God added a new dimension to my healing ministry. Often now I preach for an hour or more, then the two of us minister to the sick for four or five hours, while God bears supernatural testimony to the truth of the word I have preached. Before such sessions close, Ruth and I sometimes lay hands on other couples and transmit to them the same kind of supernatural ministry God has given us.

This expansion of our ministry has taken us on long and arduous journeys to more and more countries. We have been exposed to all the pressures caused by continual changes of climate, diet, and culture. In such situations, Ruth has foreseen my needs more quickly than I and invariably contrived amazingly ingenious ways to supply them.

In other areas, too, such as management and creative writing, God has equipped Ruth with skills that meet needs I did not even know would arise. Again and again I marvel at how her abilities complement mine, just as a glove fits a hand. Once again, as in my first marriage, God has provided me with "a helper suitable for me." In the years between my two marriages, the nature of my needs changed. But the way God has supplied them has been as faultless in my second marriage as it was in my first.

In each case, God worked according to His own plan for marriage, established at the dawn of human history. As it was with Lydia, so it has been with Ruth. God foresaw just the kind of wife I would need; He prepared her carefully for me; He placed her in the path He led me along; and He pointed her out to me as the helper that He had chosen for me.

In each case, too, the outworking of God's plan produced the union of two persons into one, which is His end purpose in marriage.

The Divine Pathway
to Marriage

4

The Gateway

In the first chapter I outlined briefly the biblical principles involved in entering into marriage; and in the next two chapters I showed how my personal experience in marriage—first with Lydia, then with Ruth—has been in amazingly accurate agreement with the biblical pattern. Since the understanding of these principles is basic to all that follows, it will be helpful at this point to recapitulate them in greater detail:

1. God Himself initiated marriage at the beginning of human history. Man had no part in planning it. Without divine revelation, man cannot understand it, much less make it a part of his experience.
2. The decision that the man was to marry proceeded from God, not from the man.
3. God knew the kind of helper that the man needed. The man did not.
4. God prepared the woman for the man.
5. God presented the woman to the man. The man did not have to go in search of her.

6. God ordained the nature of their life together. Its end purpose was unity.

7. Jesus upheld God's original plan of marriage as binding on all who would become His disciples. It is still in force today.

The standard God has thus established for marriage is high but not unattainable. There are Christians all over the world, from different races and backgrounds, who can testify that God's plan works. Any Christian willing to meet the conditions can experience its outworking in his or her own life.

What, then, are the conditions? There is one condition of unique importance, which stands like a gateway at the threshold of the life God has prepared for His people. All who would enter into His plan for their lives must pass through this gateway. This applies especially to God's plan for marriage, but it also covers every other area of the Christian life.

In Romans 12:1 Paul brings us face-to-face with this gateway: "Therefore, I urge you, brothers, in view of God's mercy, to offer your bodies as living sacrifices, holy and pleasing to God—which is your spiritual worship." In the preceding eleven chapters of Romans, Paul has expounded on the boundless mercy of God toward the human race and the full provision He has made for all men, Jew or Gentile, through the sacrificial death of Jesus Christ. Now he comes to the response God requires from each of us. It is simple and down-to-earth: Offer your body to God as a living sacrifice.

It is a sacrifice that God requires of us for His plan to work. But why does Paul emphasize that it is to be a *living* sacrifice? Because he is contrasting it with the sacrifices of the Old Testament, which were first slain and then placed dead on the altar. In the New Testament God requires each believer to offer his or her body just as totally on His altar—but it is to be a *living* body, one that is active and dedicated in His service. There is no difference in the totality of the sacrifice. In the New Testament as in the Old, God requires complete, unreserved surrender.

To offer your body to God in this way means that you no longer claim ownership or control of it. You no longer decide where it is to go, what it is to eat or wear, or what kind of service it is to perform. All that is now decided by the One to whom you have yielded complete and final control. Since He is your Creator, He knows better than you do what He can accomplish in and through that yielded body of yours.

The first result of this surrender is that it makes your body holy. In Matthew 23:19 Jesus reminds the Pharisees that it is the altar that sanctifies—or makes holy—the sacrifice placed on it, and not the other way around. This applies to your body when it is placed on God's altar. By this act it is sanctified, made holy, set apart to God.

This has a special significance for those contemplating marriage, for marriage is a union in which two *bodies* are made one. From the beginning God declared: "The two will become one *flesh.*" What a priceless privilege to bring to this union a body that has been made holy!

Unfortunately, many young people today have abused and desecrated their bodies by drugs, illicit or unnatural sex, or by many other degrading practices. Is it possible for such people to bring to the marriage union a body that has been made holy, one that is no longer a source of shame? Yes. Through the altar provided by the death of Jesus on the cross, God offers a holy body even to these. For the blood of Jesus, shed on the altar, "purifies us from every sin" (1 John 1:7).

Paul warns the Christians in Corinth that there is no place in heaven for "the sexually immoral . . . nor adulterers nor male prostitutes nor homosexual offenders . . . nor the greedy nor drunkards . . ." (1 Corinthians 6:9–10). He concludes his list by saying: "And that is what some of you were. But you were washed, you were sanctified, you were justified in the name of the Lord Jesus Christ and by the Spirit of our God" (verse 11).

Later Paul writes to the same people and says: "I promised you to one husband, to Christ, so that I might present you as *a pure virgin* to him" (2 Corinthians 11:2, italics added). What an incredible transformation Paul pictures here—from the depths of degradation to spotless righteousness and holiness! Such is the power of the blood of Jesus for those who offer their bodies upon His altar.

In Romans 12:2 Paul goes on to describe the second result of offering your body upon God's altar: "Do not conform any longer to the pattern of this world, but be transformed by the renewing of your mind. Then you will be able to test and approve what God's will is—his good, pleasing and perfect will."

In response to your surrender, God will do for you what you cannot achieve by any effort of your own will: He will renew your mind. He will change the way you think. This includes your goals, your values, your attitudes, and your priorities. All will be brought into line with those of God Himself.

This inner change will find expression in your outward behavior. You will no longer be "conformed," acting like the unregenerate people all around you. Instead, you will be "transformed," and begin to demonstrate in your conduct the very nature and character of God.

Until you begin to experience this renewal of your mind, there are many wonderful things God has planned for you that you cannot discover. In Romans 8:7 Paul calls the old, unrenewed mind "the carnal mind," which is "enmity against God: for it is not subject to the law of God, neither indeed can it be" (KJV). God will not reveal His secrets or open up

His treasures to a mind at enmity with Him. But when your mind is renewed, you will begin to discover all that God has planned for your life.

This unfolding of God's plan to your renewed mind will be progressive. Paul uses three words for it: good, pleasing, perfect.

Your first discovery will be that God's plan for you is always *good*. God never plans anything bad or harmful for any of His children. In making this discovery, you will probably have to reject the devil's lies. He will be very insistent in suggesting that full surrender to God will cost you everything that is interesting and exciting in life. He will whisper negative insinuations to your mind: "You'll have to give up everything you enjoy. . . . You'll be no better than a slave. . . . That kind of life leaves no room for fun. . . . You'll lose all your friends. . . . Your personality will never develop. . . ." and so on.

In fact, the opposite is true. Not merely is God's plan *good;* it is also *pleasing.* Full surrender to God is the gateway into a life filled with challenges and pleasures that cannot be experienced in any other way. Over the years I have met many Christians who made this kind of surrender. I have never yet met one who regretted it. I know other Christians, on the other hand, who were challenged to make this surrender and refused. Almost without exception, they ended up frustrated and unfulfilled.

As you continue to progress in your discovery of God's plan, you will go beyond the *good* and the *pleasing* to the *perfect.* Fully embraced, God's plan is perfect. Complete. There are no omissions. It covers every area of your life, meets every need, satisfies every longing.

If marriage is part of God's plan for you, then you can trust Him to work out every detail, both for you and for the mate He has destined for you. He will bring you together with a person who is so exactly suited to you that, together, you may experience marriage as God originally designed it. This will be on a level higher than the world has ever dreamed of.

Perhaps you have never made this kind of total surrender to God. You have never "offered your body to God as a living sacrifice." Perhaps you never knew God required this of you. But now you find yourself standing before this gateway—the gateway of full surrender. You long to explore all that lies on the other side, yet you are afraid. Already you begin to hear in your mind the whispered insinuations of the devil.

Let me say that I understand your feelings. More than forty years ago, I stood before the same gateway. I experienced the same inner tensions—the longing to explore all that lay on the other side; the fear of what it might cost me. My mind was flooded with questions: What will my friends say? And my family? What will happen to my university career? Finally I made the decision. I committed my whole life to God.

Never once since then have I regretted that decision or been tempted to revoke it. It opened the way into a life that has proved richer, fuller, more exciting than I had ever dreamed possible. Included in it was a mate prepared by God in each of two successive marriages. One thing I can say with full assurance: *God's plan works!*

I cannot force you through this gateway. Not even God can do that. But I can show you how to enter. All that is needed is a decision, followed by a simple prayer. If you are ready to make the decision, here is a prayer you may offer:

> *Lord Jesus Christ, I thank You that on the cross You gave Yourself as a sacrifice for my sins, so that I might be forgiven and have eternal life. In my turn, I now give myself to You. I offer my body as a living sacrifice on Your altar.*

*From now on, I belong wholly to You. Make me what
You want me to be; lead me where You want me to go.
Open up Your plan for my life.*

Now seal your decision by thanking the Lord. Thank Him
that He has heard you and received you. Thank Him that
your whole life now belongs to Him. You are His responsibility. He will open up every door of His will for you. He will
fulfill every plan and purpose He has for your life.

To all those who have made this unreserved commitment to
the Lord—either while reading these pages or at some
previous time—I can offer a guarantee: If you will read on
through this book and follow the counsel it offers concerning
marriage, you will discover what God has planned for this
area of your life, and His plan will be fulfilled. But remember,
from now on you do not make your own decisions. You find
out God's decisions and make them yours.

There is one more thing to remember, too: God gives His
best to those who leave the choice to Him.

5

Four Attitudes to Cultivate

Now that your mind is being renewed by the Holy Spirit, you are in a position to go on to the next two areas in which you will need to bring your life into line with God's requirements—your attitudes and your actions. This chapter will focus on attitudes, and the next on actions.

It is essential to put these in their right order: attitudes first, then actions. In all human conduct, attitudes precede and *determine* actions. To ignore attitudes and focus on actions is to put the cart before the horse.

This was the main emphasis of Jesus in the Sermon on the Mount. The Law of Moses focused largely on outward acts such as murder or adultery, while Jesus emphasized internal attitudes: anger, hatred, or lust in the heart. Right actions will flow inevitably from right attitudes, while wrong attitudes *cannot* produce right actions.

I believe there are attitudes in four specific areas that you need to cultivate if you want to enter into God's plan for marriage: first, your attitude toward marriage; second, your attitude toward yourself; third, your attitude toward other

people; and fourth, more specifically, your attitude toward
your parents.

Specifically, within the third of these categories, your
attitude toward other people will, of course, be a major factor
in determining your attitude toward the mate God has
appointed for you.

First, then, your attitude toward marriage. Here there are
two requirements: reverence and humility.

Are you prepared to approach marriage with the reverence
that it demands? Do you see it as a sacred mystery, formed
from eternity in the mind of God, and revealed to man for his
measureless benefit and blessing?

Every Christian who contemplates marriage should read
and reread the words of Paul in Ephesians 5:25–32:

> Husbands, love your wives, just as Christ loved the
> church and gave himself up for her to make her
> holy, cleansing her by the washing with water
> through the word, and to present her to himself as
> a radiant church, without stain or wrinkle or any
> other blemish, but holy and blameless. In this same
> way, husbands ought to love their wives as their
> own bodies. He who loves his wife loves himself.
> After all, no one ever hated his own body, but he
> feeds and cares for it, just as Christ does the
> church—for we are members of his body. "For this
> reason a man will leave his father and mother and
> be united to his wife, and the two will become one
> flesh." This is a profound mystery—but I am
> talking about Christ and the church.

Do you see what Paul is saying here? Human marriage is an
earthly counterpart of the relationship between Christ and
His Church. The union a man enjoys with his wife prefigures
the union Christ will have with His Church—a union in

which God, the Creator, and man, the creature, will be joined together in an intimate, perfect, eternal oneness. Only the supernatural grace of God can bring a man and woman together in a relationship that prefigures something so grand and so sacred.

The reverent contemplation of this mystery must inevitably bring each one of us to the place where we acknowledge: "Lord, I cannot even comprehend all you have prepared for me in marriage. Much less can I achieve it by my own efforts. Humbly, therefore, I put my hand in Yours and ask You to teach me and to guide me."

If you will make this your attitude, you can rest in the assurance of Psalm 25:9: "[God] guides the humble in what is right and teaches them his way." In His own way and time, God will place the key in your hand.

Perhaps at this point you feel inclined to say, "This is too high for me—too difficult. I'm neither worthy nor capable of it."

Such a reaction is not necessarily wrong. Countless unhappy marriages have resulted from people entering into them without giving serious consideration to all that would be required of them. Unfortunately, this is true not only of unbelievers. It includes many Christians.

At this point, however, you are faced with the second main issue: your attitude toward yourself.

A sense of self-worth is one of the most important elements in your making a success of your life, not least in marriage. Also, it is one of the many priceless benefits available to you through your faith in Christ. But perhaps you have not yet discovered this.

Many personal problems may come to mind: "I had an unhappy childhood." "My parents were divorced." "I've never made a success of anything." "I don't feel comfortable with other people, especially the opposite sex." "I really don't see what life holds for me." And so on.

All that may be true; but if you are a Christian, it is no longer relevant. Listen to what Paul says: "Therefore, if anyone is in Christ, he is a new creation; the old has gone, the new has come!" (2 Corinthians 5:17). Through the new birth you have become a *new creation*. God did not take you as you were and then simply make a few adjustments and improvements. He made you new all over, from the inside out. As far as God is concerned, your past sins and failures are not merely forgiven; the record of them has been completely erased. You have been given a totally new start. It is up to you to accept this in faith and act accordingly.

In the natural order, a person's primary basis for self-acceptance and self-worth lies in the love, care, and discipline received from parents. With this kind of background, he is secure in his identity. He knows who he is and where he came from. Since World War II, however, much of this has been changed by delinquent or emasculated fathers, and by mothers who either have become equally delinquent or have struggled unsuccessfully to fill the roles of both father and mother. As a result, we are faced with a generation of unparented children who have grown to adulthood carrying within them a paralyzing sense of inadequacy and insecurity.

This is one main reason for the breakdown of many marriages and other close relationships. Insecure people are difficult to live with. They cannot rest in a relationship, but are in continual need of something to bolster their self-esteem. Yet nothing suffices for long. Such people do not know how to receive love, and therefore they cannot give it. The second of the two Great Commandments charges us to love our neighbor as we love ourselves. If we have not learned to love ourselves, we have nothing to offer to our neighbor.

Through faith in Christ, God has provided a divine remedy for this condition so prevalent in today's world. He has become our heavenly Father. He has adopted us personally as

His children. He has made us "accepted in the beloved"—
that is, in Jesus. We are no longer waifs or orphans. We are
no longer aliens or strangers. We belong to the best family in
the universe, the family of God. And because God has
accepted us, we can accept ourselves. To do anything less is
plain unbelief.

Legally, all this is fully true from the moment we are born
again. Experientially, however, we need to cultivate an ever-
expanding realization of what we have become in the family
of God. To achieve this requires long hours spent gazing into
the mirror of God's Word. Here we come to see for ourselves,
stage by stage and detail by detail, what it means to be a child
of God. As we gaze into this divine mirror, the Spirit of God
works within us, transforming us into the likeness of what we
are looking at.

This is the process Paul describes in 2 Corinthians 3:18:
"But we all, with unveiled face beholding as in a mirror the
glory of the Lord, are being transformed into the same image
from glory to glory, just as from the Lord, the Spirit" (NASB).

Once you have established a proper attitude toward
yourself, based on your relationship to God as your Father,
you are ready to consider the third main issue: your
relationships with other people.

At the beginning of human history, man's rebellion against
God and his consequent fall shut him up into a narrow prison
of self. From that time on, self-centeredness has been one of
the most obvious effects of the devil's influence in a human
life. In ministering deliverance to those afflicted by evil spirits,
I have observed that such people are nearly always intensely
self-centered. They delight to sit for hours in counseling
sessions and to expatiate in wearisome detail on all their
problems. They fail to realize that the more they talk about
themselves, the stronger they make the bars of their own
prison.

One great effect of redemption through Christ is our release from this prison of self. Identification with Christ enables us to relate to other people as He did. In simple, down-to-earth language Paul explains how this works: "Don't just think about your own affairs, but be interested in others, too, and in what they are doing. Your attitude should be the kind that was shown us by Jesus Christ . . ." (Philippians 2:4–5, LB).

There are two basic causes of broken or unhappy marriages: lack of consideration and lack of sensitivity, in one or both parties. This in turn leads to a breakdown in communication.

These basic problems may manifest themselves in various kinds of behavior, depending on the temperaments of those involved. Some of the most obvious manifestations are sexual unfaithfulness; arguing and quarreling; each of the parties going his or her own way and building a separate, independent life. All these manifestations have one thing in common: they frustrate the end purpose of God in marriage, which is unity.

The grace of God in redemption offers us two positive antidotes: appreciation and thankfulness. Appreciation is the inward reaction, and thankfulness the outward expression. Together they act as a lubricant that can keep two people flowing together in harmony with one another.

So cultivate both! Approach every situation and every relationship with a positive attitude. Look for anything that is good, small or great. When you find the good, make sure you express your appreciation of it. This will make you the kind of person who is easy to live with. Practice this in all your relationships as you go through life, and in due course you will reap the benefits in a harmonious marriage.

Let us suppose you have been praying earnestly for a mate and your heavenly Father has heard your prayer. You can trust, therefore, that He is preparing for you exactly the mate that you need, right in every detail. But because He is such a loving Father, He will not commit one of His precious children to you as a mate until He has assured Himself that you will treat her (or him) as every child of God deserves to be treated.

There remains one more important attitude to consider: your attitude toward your parents. You may be surprised to find this included in the requirements for a successful marriage. Nevertheless, it belongs here.

The apostle Paul quotes the fifth of the Ten Commandments and comments on it as follows:

> Children, obey your parents in the Lord, for this is right. "Honor your father and mother"—which is the first commandment with a promise—"that it may go well with you and that you may enjoy long life on the earth."
>
> (Ephesians 6:1–3)

Paul points out that the preceding four commandments had no promise attached to the keeping of them. But to this fifth commandment, relating to parents, God added a special promise: "That it may go well with you. . . ." At the same time, the promise implies a condition: If you want it to go well with you, you must be careful to honor your parents. Conversely, if you do not honor your parents, you cannot expect it to go well with you.

Bear in mind that it is possible to honor your parents without agreeing with them on all points or endorsing everything they do. You may disagree strongly with them in some matters, yet maintain a respectful attitude toward them. To honor your parents in this way is also to honor God Himself, who gave this commandment.

I am convinced that a proper attitude toward parents is an

essential requirement for God's blessing on any person's life. In all the years I have dealt with Christians in teaching, pastoring, counseling, and other relationships, I have never met one who had a wrong attitude toward his parents and enjoyed the blessing of God. Such a person may be zealous in many areas of the Christian life, active in the church, energetic in ministry. He may have a place in heaven waiting for him. Yet there is always something lacking in his life: the blessing and favor of God.

I have seen many Christians, on the other hand, whose lives were revolutionized when they acknowledged a wrong attitude toward parents, repented of it, and made the necessary changes. I remember one man who was convicted of a lifetime of bitterness and hatred toward his father. Although his father was already dead, this man journeyed hundreds of miles to the cemetery where his father was buried. Kneeling beside the grave, he poured out his heart to God in deep contrition and repentance. He did not rise from his knees until he knew his sin was forgiven and he was released from its evil effects. From that point on, the whole course of his life changed from frustration and defeat to victory and fulfillment.

Many young couples struggle with problems in their marriage that they cannot trace to their source. They are committed to the Lord and to one another. There is genuine love between them. Yet there is an indefinable something missing, which is God's favor. In such cases, I always recommend that they examine their attitudes toward their parents and make any changes that Scripture requires. Often this has changed a struggling marriage into a successful one.

In this age of delinquent parents, it must be acknowledged that many young people have legitimate grievances. Often they have grown up in divided, strife-torn homes, without any of the love or care or discipline that every child has a right to expect from parents. Nevertheless, this does not justify wrong attitudes of resentment or rebellion. Furthermore, such attitudes are extremely harmful to those who harbor them—more deadly, in the long run, than a physical disease like cancer.

Once I counseled a young man who was engaged to a lovely Christian girl. He sincerely loved his fiancee, yet at times his attitude toward her would change to one of hatred and rage, bordering on violence. To his surprise, I began to question him about his attitude toward his father, rather than toward his fiancee.

He admitted that he hated his father and had rebelled against him since childhood. I persuaded him to confess this as a sin, to lay down his rebellion, and to forgive his father. From that time on, he had no more problems in relating to his fiancee. Had he not been released from his wrong attitude toward his father, it would ultimately have ruined his marriage.

In the final analysis, cultivating a right attitude toward parents does not necessarily indicate a high level of spirituality. It is merely enlightened self-interest.

"Suppose my parents ask me to do something wrong, something contrary to the Bible," a young person may ask. "Does that mean I have to obey them?"

The answer to this is an emphatic *no*. If there really is a clear-cut choice between obeying God and obeying parents, our response must be that of Peter before the Sanhedrin: "We must obey God rather than men!" (Acts 5:29). If, on the other hand, it is merely a question of a young person laying down his self-will in an issue where no disobedience to God is involved, then the requirement to obey parents still stands.

The primary issue, however, is not obedience but submission. Obedience is an *act*, but submission is an *attitude*. Even in a situation in which a young Christian decides that to obey parents would be to disobey God, he can still maintain an attitude of submission. He can say to his parents, "In this case, my conscience does not allow me to do what you ask of me, but I still respect and honor you."

It often happens that a young person's attitude of respectful submission will bring about a change in his parents' attitude. Submissiveness paves the way for God to intervene, while stubbornness shuts Him out.

In conclusion, remember the warning of Jesus in Mark 4:24: "With the measure you use, it will be measured to you—and even more." The way you relate to others—parents, family, friends, fellow Christians—will determine the way they relate to you. More important still, it will determine the way God relates to you. The same measure that you use will be measured back to you.

6

Eight Guidelines To Follow

Have you given careful attention to the basic *attitudes* that will enable you to build a successful marriage? If so, it is now time for you to consider the kinds of *actions* you need to practice in daily living, if you are to find and follow the path that leads to the marriage you desire. This chapter lists eight such actions, all of them based on Scripture.

Before you start to read them, however, you need to understand that they are not intended as a set of hard-and-fast rules. Success in the Christian life is not achieved merely by making and keeping rules. In fact, people who live it that way usually encounter frustration. The reason is that they have not grasped the difference between law and grace.

Law operates through a set of external rules, engraved on tablets of stone. Grace operates through laws written by the Holy Spirit within the human heart. Only the Holy Spirit, who is called "the finger of God," can reach into the recesses of the human heart and write there the laws of life. Apart from the Holy Spirit, grace cannot operate and Christianity becomes merely a system of morality, one too high for any human being to achieve by his own efforts.

My mind goes back to the home in Ramallah where Lydia and I first lived after we were married. In one corner of the living room stood a potted creeping plant with delicate, glossy leaves. In Arabic it was called *dahabiya*—the "golden one." Over the years it had grown up the wall in the corner where it was planted and spread right across the ceiling to the opposite corner.

Lydia had trained it to grow that way by a very simple device. In the path she wanted the plant to follow—first up the wall and then across the ceiling—she had driven in small nails with their heads protruding a fraction of an inch. By some instinct built into it by the Creator, the plant reached out a tendril to each successive nail, coiled itself around it, then reached onward to the next nail. Thus, the nails determined the path of the plant's upward and onward growth.

I would like you to use the successive teachings in this chapter just as that plant used the nails in the wall and ceiling. View them not as rules but as guidelines. By the prompting and power of the Holy Spirit within you, reach out to each successive guideline. Practice it in your daily living until you have a firm grasp upon it. Then reach out to each of the succeeding guidelines in turn. And bear in mind that this will take much ongoing prayer.

In Ecclesiastes 12:11 Solomon uses a similar picture of the kind of teaching he provided for God's people: "The words of the wise are like goads, their collected sayings like firmly embedded nails—given by one Shepherd."

As you turn now to these guidelines, view them in that way: as goads to spur you on in your Christian life, and as nails you can reach up to and hold onto with the tendrils of your faith. Remember, too, that they are all given by one Shepherd, the Lord Jesus, the Shepherd of your soul, who loves you and has made full provision for your well-being.

Guideline No. 1: "Your word is a lamp to my feet and a light for my path" (Psalm 119:105).

David describes here how we may find God's pathway for us through life. The light we need is provided by God's Word. As long as we practice obedience to that Word in every situation, we will never stray from the path God has appointed for us. We may not be able to see where that path is taking us, but we can rest assured that in God's time it will bring us out to the fulfillment of His plan for our lives.

As I have written elsewhere:

> There will be times when the world around us will be in total darkness. We will not be able to see more than a few feet in any direction. There may be unsolved problems ahead. There may be dangers around the corner, but in the midst of it all we have this guarantee: if we are sincerely obeying the Word of God as it is revealed to us in any given situation, we will never walk in the dark. We will never put our foot in some treacherous place that will cause us to stumble and fall into injury or disaster.
>
> This guarantee, however, applies only to one specific area: the place where we are to plant our next footstep. God does not promise us that we will be able to see more than one step ahead. Beyond that, we may have no way of knowing what awaits us—but that is not our concern. All that God requires of us is to take the next step of simple obedience to His Word.
>
> Our greatest danger is that we will seek to peer too far ahead into the darkness. In so doing we may

miss the place for our next step, which is the only area illuminated for us at that moment.*

Rest assured, then: Obedience to God's Word will keep you in the path that leads to the marriage He has planned for you.

Guideline No. 2: "But if we walk in the light, as he is in the light, we have fellowship with one another . . ." (I John 1:7).

This guideline follows naturally after the previous one, which dealt with walking in the light of God's Word. This one deals with the consequence of walking in that light: "We have fellowship with one another." Obedience to God's Word automatically brings Christians together and enables them to relate to one another.

The opposite is also true. Christians who do not enjoy fellowship with other Christians are not walking in the light. There is some area in their lives in which they are not obeying God's Word. The only exceptions would be Christians who, through circumstances outside their control, are cut off from fellowship with other Christians. This was true in my case for months on end in the North African deserts. Another example is Christians imprisoned for their faith.

Apart from such exceptions, however, fellowship with other believers is essential to success and progress in the Christian life. It is both the test and the result of walking in the light of God's Word.

If we do not cultivate fellowship with other believers, with whom are we to have fellowship? There really is only one alternative: with unbelievers. The Bible strongly warns us against this:

---

*Quoted from *Chords from David's Harp*, 1983, published by Chosen/Zondervan.

Do not be yoked together with unbelievers. For
what do righteousness and wickedness have in
common? Or what fellowship can light have with
darkness? What harmony is there between Christ
and Belial? What does a believer have in common
with an unbeliever?

(2 Corinthians 6:14–15)

Paul is not telling us to be cold or hostile toward our non-
Christian neighbors. He is simply warning us that we cannot
afford to establish with unbelievers the close relationships that
are appropriate with believers. Obviously, he has in mind
various kinds of relationships. But the first word he uses—
yoke—is used regularly for the marriage relationship. First
and foremost, Paul is warning that *it is always wrong for a
Christian to marry a non-Christian.*

I cannot say this too emphatically to every unmarried
Christian who reads these pages: You are not free to marry a
non-Christian. You are not even free to entertain the thought.
Make up your mind from this moment on, if you have not
already done so, that marriage with an unbeliever is outside of
God's plan for your life.

The best protection against wrong relationships is right
relationships. Be diligent, then, to cultivate fellowship and
friendship with fellow believers. In most cases, marriage
develops out of existing relationships. If you have built strong
relationships with other Christians, you are not likely even to
contemplate marriage with a non-Christian.

Your safest course is to decide right now about the kinds of
relationships you are going to cultivate. Then affirm your
decision to the Lord in the words of the psalmist: "I am a
friend to all who fear you, to all who follow your precepts"
(Psalm 119:63).

Guideline No. 3: ". . . Those who are led by the Spirit of God are sons of God" (Romans 8:14).

The New Testament indicates two different ways the Holy Spirit works to make us members of God's family. First, in order to become God's children, we must be born again of His Spirit. Then, in order to become mature sons of God, we must be led by His Spirit. Many Christians who have been born again of the Holy Spirit have never learned to be led by Him. Consequently, they never grow to true spiritual maturity or find God's fullest plan for their lives.

Consider how this applies to your need to find the right mate. Let us say you live in the United States, a nation of nearly 300 million people. Or you may live in Britain, with 56 million people. Among all these millions, God is preparing one specific person to be your mate. It may well be a person you have not yet met, whose name you do not even know. Add to that the possibility that your appointed mate may not even live in the same country (which was true in each of my marriages). How are you to find that person? The proverbial picture of searching for a needle in a haystack scarcely does justice to the complexity of the problem.

God's Word indicates the answer: to be led by the Holy Spirit. He alone knows who and where the person is whom God has appointed as your mate. You must learn, therefore, how to allow the Holy Spirit to lead you.

For this, there are two key words: *dependence* and *sensitivity*. First, acknowledge your total dependence on the Holy Spirit. If He does not guide you, you will miss God's purpose. Cultivate the habit of seeking His direction in every situation and every decision, small or great. Sometimes the decisions you think unimportant are the most important of all, and vice versa. Seeking the Holy Spirit's direction does not necessarily involve using a lot of religious language in prayer. It may often mean just turning momentarily to Him with an inward thought.

Second, cultivate sensitivity to the Holy Spirit. He is not a drill sergeant. He does not shout orders at you. His prompting is usually gentle. He speaks with "a still, small voice." If your ears are not tuned to it, you will not hear Him.

Let me recommend a specific prayer Ruth and I pray almost every day: "Lord, help us to be always in the right place at the right time." We pray this with the knowledge that only the Holy Spirit can make it happen.

And the results are often interesting! One afternoon, while our daughter Jesika was living with us in Jerusalem, Ruth and I walked into the center of the city to do some shopping. As we walked along the main street, I said to Ruth, "I feel we should cross over to the other side." We did so and continued walking. Within one minute, we ran into a married couple who were friends of Jesika. They were in Jerusalem for just half-a-day and wanted to get in touch with her, but did not have our address or phone number. Meanwhile, Jesika was at home, feeling the need for Christian fellowship.

Through that encounter, Jesika's friends were able to get in touch with her, and they enjoyed an evening of fellowship together. The encounter would not have taken place if Ruth and I had not crossed the street just at that moment. Who prompted us to do that? The Holy Spirit, of course!

Imagine yourself in a somewhat similar situation. You are driving down the street looking for a place to get a hamburger. There are two places on opposite sides of the street. Serving in one of them is a young person you have never met, but whom God is preparing to be your mate. "Something" nudges your hand on the steering wheel, and you turn into the parking lot of the place on the left. Inside, you strike up an acquaintance with a young person who, like you, has been praying for the mate of God's choice. In due course, you discover this was God's appointment for you both.

Who was it that "nudged" your hand? The Holy Spirit. But if you had not responded to that nudge, you might have missed God's plan for your life. It is not enough, then, merely to pray. You must also allow the Holy Spirit to guide you to the answer to your prayer.

Sometimes the Holy Spirit guides us in ways that are dramatic and supernatural. At other times He works through a nudge or a whisper. We must be open to both. If we are not open to the supernatural, we set arbitrary limits to God's plan for our lives. He may have planned something so far beyond our natural expectations that it can only be revealed to us supernaturally—by a vision, for example, or a prophecy. If we look only for the dramatic and the supernatural, on the other hand, we may miss the gentle nudge or the whisper. It is not for us to decide in advance how the Holy Spirit will work. We must be sensitive to Him no matter how He guides us.

Guideline No. 4: "Above all else, guard your heart, for it is the wellspring of life" (Proverbs 4:23).

There is an area central to human personality and decisive to human destiny, which the Bible calls the *heart*. Whatever rules your heart will determine the course of your life. You need to guard your heart, therefore, more carefully than any other area of your being. This applies particularly to those impulses and emotions related to sex.

Be continually watchful, first of all, concerning what you allow *into* your heart. In our contemporary culture, young people in particular are being bombarded continually with influences that undermine biblical standards for sex and marriage. These are at work through teaching in schools and colleges, through the media, through peer pressure, and through other ways that are hard to detect. If you are to find God's plan for marriage in your life, you must set a guard over your heart that refuses admission to all unbiblical and anti-Christian standards.

Another influence to guard against is that of fantasy. At a certain period in adolescence it is common to indulge in a good deal of daydreaming. But do not allow this to develop into a habit of fantasizing. If you are prone to this, resist it firmly and force yourself to face up to reality. Otherwise, you will come to a point where is is hard to distinguish between fantasy and reality. And when it comes to marriage, you will have formed an unreal, subjective image of the person who is to be your mate.

This can affect you in one of two ways. First, the mate God has appointed for you may not correspond with the image of your fantasy, and you may be unwilling to accept His choice. Or you may impose the image of your fantasy upon a real person and marry that person—only to discover, after marriage, that the real person is totally different from the one you imagined, and not the one God selected for you at all.

Be no less careful concerning what you release *out of* your heart. Don't indulge in flirtations or superficial relationships with the opposite sex. It may seem exciting to stir someone's emotions and allow your own to be stirred, but one day you may discover that your emotions have gotten out of your control. Like the sorcerer's apprentice, who discovered the formula to release the water in a flood but did not know the formula to recall it, you may discover you have released emotions you are not able to recall. The result is an emotional entanglement with a person who is in no way suited to be your mate.

Here is a safe rule to follow. First, discover the mate God has chosen for you. Then, release your emotions toward that person. In this way, you will not need to recall the flood.

Guideline No. 5: "Since ancient times no one has heard, no ear has perceived, no eye has seen any God besides you, who acts on behalf of those who wait for him" (Isaiah 64:4).

You may find this the hardest guideline of all to embrace: *Be prepared to wait!* Isaiah tells us in the passage quoted above that in all the universe there is only one true God, and one of His distinctive characteristics is that He "acts on behalf of those who wait for Him."

It is not the case that God always requires all His children to wait for the mate of His choice. There are those who find their mate early in life and enter without delay into a successful marriage that lasts a lifetime. This is one of those areas in which each of us must bow before the sovereignty of God. If He unites us quickly with our appointed mate, we praise Him. If He requires us to wait, we praise Him just the same. God deals with each one of us according to His knowledge of us and according to His special plan for each life.

If you are one of those whom God requires to wait, be encouraged by the fact that God has required many of His choicest servants to wait long periods for the fulfillment of His promise or purpose. Abraham waited until he was 100 for the birth of Isaac, his promised son. Moses waited eighty years, forty of them in the desert, to become the deliverer of Israel. David waited about fifteen years from the time he was first anointed king until the kingdom became his. Israel waited many long centuries for their Messiah. The Church has waited nearly two millennia for the return of Jesus—and is still waiting.

God uses waiting to work out various purposes in our lives. First, waiting tests our faith. Only those who really believe in God's provision are prepared to wait for it. The apostle Peter warns us that just as gold is refined by fire, so faith must be refined by testing (see 1 Peter 1:6–7). Only faith that passes the test is accepted by God as genuine.

Second, waiting purifies our motives. If God requires you to wait for your mate, you need to ask yourself: Why am I eager to marry? Is it because God wants it for me, or because I want it for myself? Am I motivated by God's will or by self-will? Waiting will supply you with the answer to your own question.

Third, waiting builds our character to maturity. James tells us: ". . . The testing of your faith develops perseverance. Perseverance must finish its work so that you may be mature and complete . . ." (James 1:3–4). A person who has learned to wait is no longer at the mercy of fluctuating moods and emotions. He or she has acquired confidence and stability. In God's time, these characteristics will prove of inestimable value in building a strong, successful marriage.

Guideline No. 6: "I tell you the truth, unless a kernel of wheat falls to the ground and dies, it remains only a single seed. But if it dies, it produces many seeds" (John 12:24).

Jesus is unfolding a principle that works throughout nature, and also in the lives of God's people. Briefly stated, it warns us: *Be prepared for death and resurrection.*

Like the previous guideline, this one does not apply to all who find God's plan for marriage. In my case, it applied to my second marriage but not to my first. I include it here because I have learned from experience how important it is. After I met Ruth, I knew God had placed in my heart a "seed" of love for her, yet I had to watch it fall into the ground and die. If I had not understood and accepted this principle, I might never have had the faith to press through into the resurrection God had prepared for us.

As I wrestled at that time with God's dealings in my life, I cried out, "Lord, why do You give us something and then ask for it back again? Why do so many of the things You bless have to pass through death and resurrection?"

I felt God gave me the following answer: *Because when I resurrect something, I resurrect it the way I want it to be, not the way it was originally.*

Certainly that was true of the relationship between Ruth and me. Passing through death and resurrection gave it a depth and security it would never otherwise have had. If God should take you through a similar experience, I trust that our testimony may give you the encouragement you need.

Guideline No. 7: "The way of a fool seems right to him, but a wise man listens to advice" (Proverbs 12:15). "A fool spurns his father's discipline, but whoever heeds correction shows prudence" (Proverbs 15:5).

I have already emphasized, in my chapter on cultivating the right attitudes, the importance of the blessing of parents. This provides a foundation on which to build success in every area of life, especially in marriage. Even if you and your parents do not see eye-to-eye in every matter, it is worth exercising much patience and self-restraint in order to build on the foundation of their blessing.

Over and above the special blessing of parents, it is important for you as a young person to seek the counsel of godly men such as pastors or other church leaders, who are older than you in years and in the faith. Such men have already traversed the road that lies ahead of you. They know its snares and its dangers. Also, they have had opportunity to scale some of the mountains and thus to get a wider view of the countryside. You can benefit much from their perspective.

There is a tendency among young people today to turn only to their peers for counsel. But the counsel peers have to offer is based mainly on theory, or at best head knowledge. They have still to prove in experience that their theories really work. It is a mark of wisdom and humility to seek counsel from older people who have achieved success in the areas of life where you need guidance. If you make a regular practice of doing this, it will help to keep your feet in the path leading to the fulfillment of God's plan for you.

Guideline No. 8: ". . . A prudent wife is from the Lord" (Proverbs 19:14). "He who finds a wife finds what is good and receives favor from the Lord" (Proverbs 18:22).

In these proverbs, two truths are intertwined: First, it is the Lord who bestows the gift of a prudent wife; and second, this gift is a mark of His special favor on the one who receives it. Solomon presents these truths from the perspective of the man, but it is obvious that the corollary is true for the woman. For her, too, the gift of the right mate comes from the Lord and is a mark of His favor.

This leads to an important, practical conclusion for both man and woman. If you want the Lord to give you the kind of mate you need, there is one thing you must do above all others: You must diligently cultivate the Lord's favor. His satisfaction must be your highest ambition. Approach every situation and decision, then, with one primary question: What will please the Lord? If you are diligent to seek what gives the Lord pleasure, He in turn will provide for you what gives you pleasure.

David describes this approach to life and the response it calls forth from the Lord: "Delight yourself in the Lord and he will give you the desires of your heart" (Psalm 37:4). If you find your highest satisfaction in God Himself, He will respond in two ways. First, He will implant in your heart those desires that correspond to His highest will for you. Then He will guide you to their fulfillment.

All the previous seven guidelines can be summed up in this final one: Make God's favor the supreme objective of living, and you can confidently leave to Him the choice, the preparation, and the provision of your mate.

7

A Man Prepares for Marriage

To pass from the single to the married state is one of the most important and challenging transitions that can take place in a person's life. Anyone who wants to do it successfully will make careful and thorough preparation. To attempt such a transition without adequate preparation is like jumping into deep water without first learning to swim. The results are usually disastrous!

Anyone preparing for a trade or profession, such as carpentry or medicine, needs a clear picture of what he intends to become before he starts the preparation. The same is true for marriage. A person preparing for marriage needs a clear picture of the role he or she will be required to fill.

For obvious reasons, the preparation a man needs to make for marriage differs from the preparation a woman needs to make. In this chapter I will outline the main preparations I believe a man should make. In the next chapter Ruth will do the same for women. Each of us speaks out of the experience of two marriages.

What is the role of a man in marriage? In the ordinary

course of events, the initial role of husband is a stepping-stone to a second, equally challenging role—that of father. These two roles may be combined under the single description *head of a family*.

Paul presents this concept of headship by linking it to the nature of God Himself and to relationships within the Godhead: "Now I want you to realize that the head of every man is Christ, and the head of the woman is man, and the head of Christ is God" (1 Corinthians 11:3).

Paul pictures a descending chain of headship, which starts in heaven and ends in the family: God the Father is the head of Christ; Christ is the head of the man (husband); and the man (husband) is the head of the woman (wife).

In this chain, Christ and the husband each have a double relationship—to the one above and to the one below. Thus, Christ represents God the Father (above Him) to the man (below Him); and the man, in turn, represents Christ (above him) to his wife (below him).

Here is a clear scriptural picture of the role of the husband who also becomes a father: *he represents Christ to his wife and family*. What a tremendous responsibility—and what a sacred privilege!

How can you prepare yourself to meet this awesome challenge?

The key to the life of Jesus was His relationship to the Father. He expressed this in various ways: "The Son can do nothing by himself; he can do only what he sees his Father doing, because whatever the Father does the Son also does" (John 5:19). "Anyone who has seen me has seen the Father. . . . The words I say to you are not just my own. Rather, it is the Father, living in me, who is doing his work" (John 14:9–10).

In like manner, your success as head of your family will depend on your relationship to Jesus. Make Him the source of your words and actions. Rely on His strength and wisdom within you, not on your own. Let Him live out His life through you.

What are some of the facets of His life that will most appropriately be revealed in you, as a husband and father?

First of all, Jesus is the Lover and the Bridegroom of His Church. All His other ministries flow out of the deep, pure fountain of His love. Allow Him to open up this fountain within your heart. Don't be afraid of being tender. It is a mark of strength, not weakness. "Love is as strong as death" (Song of Songs 8:6). "[Love] always protects, always trusts, always hopes, always perseveres. Love never fails . . ." (1 Corinthians 13:7–8).

Consider the tenderness with which the Lord speaks to Israel in Jeremiah 31:3: "I have loved you with an everlasting love; I have drawn you with loving-kindness." It is by this tenderness that Jesus draws His people to Himself. Allow Him to impart a measure of it to you. Through it He will draw your bride to you just as He draws the Church to Himself.

In our modern, high-powered, cynical society, there is very little left of real tenderness. It has become almost a forgotten quality. Yet there is something in every woman that longs for it. She will respond to it just as a flower opens its petals to the sun.

Tenderness goes hand-in-hand with romance. If you want a picture of the two combined, study the Song of Songs. This beautiful, often neglected book has much to teach God's people about love, both divine and human. I remember Lydia once remarking, "Any time I feel drawn to the Song of Songs, I know I am on a high level in my spiritual life."

In the weeks before I married Ruth, I read the Song of Songs several times. I studied the various parts—the lover, the Shulammite, the friends. I believe this helped to build the kind of relationship that Ruth and I enjoy.

Romance is not some special kind of activity on its own. It is a quality imparted to other activities that makes them more exciting and enjoyable. This may be illustrated from something so simple as eating a meal. Romance is not an extra course tacked onto the end of the meal. It is a seasoning added to every course. It can impart that extra flavor of excitement to even commonplace activities like a shopping expedition, a drive to church, or an evening stroll.

Let me speak for a moment from personal experience. I have helped to raise nine daughters from different racial backgrounds. I have been married twice. I am familiar with cultures and lifestyles from many parts of the globe. I do not believe there is a woman anywhere in the world who does not appreciate romance and tenderness. Why should you settle for a drab marriage? Follow the pattern of Jesus, and aim for a marriage that will be like the one He is planning with His Church.

Another quality of the love of Jesus is that it is self-giving. ". . . Christ loved the church and gave himself up for her" (Ephesians 5:25). A successful marriage must follow that pattern. It consists of two lives laid down for each other. First the husband, like Jesus, lays down his life for the wife. Then the wife in her turn, like the Church, lays down her life for the husband. Thereafter, each finds fulfillment in the life of the other. The key to this kind of relationship is the understanding that scriptural marriage is based on a covenant.*

Self-giving is not natural, however, to fallen human nature. It needs to be cultivated. First it requires a decision. Then it must be worked out in daily living, until it becomes part of your character. Do not wait until marriage to begin to give of

---

*I have explained how this works in my book *The Marriage Covenant*, published by Derek Prince Ministries, Fort Lauderdale, Florida (1978).

yourself. That can lead to much unnecessary suffering for you and your wife.

When I married Lydia, I had very little experience of the give-and-take of close personal relationships, because I had no brothers or sisters. Looking back, I realize this caused unnecessary problems for Lydia and the children. I thank God for the grace He gave all of us to work through those problems. Thirty-three years later, when I married Ruth, I told her she was getting a much better prepared husband than Lydia had started out with!

Your marriage will benefit greatly if you learn to give of yourself now in the relationships you have with those around you. If you still live at home, give of yourself there in small acts of service. Take out the garbage even when it is not your turn. Help with the dishes so your sister can go out with her friend. Babysit your younger brother so your parents can have an evening out by themselves.

In the context of church life, too, there are many opportunities for service. Visit the shut-ins. Wash the pastor's car. Volunteer to clean the sanctuary on Saturday morning. Help a widow or handicapped person with grocery shopping. All these seemingly small acts will help to build in you something of the self-giving nature of Jesus, which will one day enrich your marriage and make you a pattern to your own children.

The picture of Jesus as Bridegroom in Ephesians 5:25–26 brings out another aspect of His ministry—that of Teacher. He gave Himself up for the Church "to make her holy, cleansing her by the washing with water through the word." The teaching of God's Word must make the Church pure and holy, fit to be Christ's Bride.

Here is another way you will be able to represent Jesus to your wife and family: Make provision for them to receive the kind of Bible teaching that will fit them to be part of His Bride. If God blesses your home with children, teaching them will be one of your most important tasks. "Fathers, do not exasperate your children; instead, bring them up in the training and instruction of the Lord" (Ephesians 6:4).

In many families today, what Bible teaching there is often falls to the mother. This is contrary to divine order. The mother certainly has her part to play, but the primary responsibility rests on the father. In a home where only the mother gives the spiritual instruction, the boys are likely to conclude that "the Bible is a woman's book." When they reach adolescence, they may well decide it has nothing further to offer them.

How can you prepare yourself to fill the role of teacher in your home?

First of all, acquire an overall knowledge of the Bible. If possible, attend a local church where sound Bible teaching is given. This may be supplemented in various ways: books, cassettes, correspondence courses, seminars, conferences, radio teaching programs, and so on.

From this, go on to systematic, in-depth study of the great basic doctrines of the Christian faith. You will need this solid foundation to build on. Concentrate on such books as Romans, Galatians, Ephesians, Hebrews. Various kinds of material are available from the same sources listed above. Be prepared for hard work!

At the same time, ask God to open a door for you to some situation in which you can begin to share with others the knowledge you are gaining. There are various possibilities: a home group, a group of college students, a Sunday school class, an inner-city mission. Teaching others is the best way to find out how much you have really learned yourself.

All this will prepare you to fill the role of teacher in your own home. By now you should be qualified to teach the basic truths yourself. Beyond this, through your own studies, you will have discovered other sources of teaching, such as those mentioned above. Draw on these in order to build on the foundation of biblical knowledge that you have been able to lay in the lives of your family.

Closely related to the ministry of Jesus as Teacher is His priestly ministry as Intercessor. The writer of Hebrews tells us that after His ascension, Jesus entered the inner sanctuary, behind the second curtain, to appear there as High Priest on our behalf: "Therefore he is able to save completely those who come to God through him, because he always lives to intercede for them" (Hebrews 7:25).

In representing Jesus to your wife and family, you must learn to combine the roles of priestly intercessor and teacher. As teacher, you will represent God to your family. As intercessor, you will represent your family to God. There is no higher ministry open to you. Here are some ways to prepare yourself for it.

First, study carefully the biblical patterns of this kind of intercessory ministry. Trace the results it produced in each situation. The following are some outstanding examples: Abraham interceding on behalf of his nephew Lot and the city of Sodom (Genesis 18:16–33); Moses interceding on behalf of Israel after they had made and worshiped a golden calf (Exodus 32:1–14); Moses and Aaron interceding on behalf of the Israelites dying of a plague (Numbers 16:41–50).

Meditate on the implications of what God said concerning Israel in Ezekiel 22:30: "I looked for a man among them who would build up the wall and stand before me in the gap on behalf of the land so I would not have to destroy it, but I found none." Wherever God places you, you can learn to be "a man who stands in the gap" on behalf of others.

You will find it inspiring, too, to memorize the priestly blessing that Aaron and his sons were instructed to pronounce on their fellow Israelites (Numbers 6:24–27). When

you become a priest over your family, you will have a pattern
for blessing them, which will be one of your greatest
privileges!

The second way to prepare yourself for the role of priestly
intercessor is to cultivate a regular personal prayer life (if you
have not already done so). Be systematic; devote your best
time to it. Ask God to lay on your heart the individuals for
whom He wants you to intercede. These may be members of
your family or your church, workmates, or other associates.
You should also include God's ministering servants who have
helped you and are likewise helping others. It is often
practical to make a list of the people for whom you pray
regularly. Accept personal responsibility before God for them.

Third, participate regularly in some kind of prayer meeting.
Learning to pray with others will help you to overcome self-
consciousness and will better equip you to pray in due course
with your wife and your family. Prayer should become as
natural a part of your family life as meals or play.

There is one important extra benefit resulting from learning
the ministry of priestly intercession: It will help you greatly in
the other roles in which you seek to represent Jesus. In fact,
your success in the ministry of prayer will probably determine
the extent of your success in those other areas.

The best summary of your responsibilities as Jesus' repre-
sentative in your home is contained in the concept introduced
at the beginning of this chapter: *headship*. In practical terms,
what does this tell you about your role?

Let me answer by asking another question: What is the
function of a *physical* head in relation to the rest of the body?
It takes three forms: receiving input from every area of the
body; making decisions; giving direction. Every part of the
body has the right to communicate with the head, but the
head is responsible to assimilate the information it receives
and then to initiate the appropriate action.

Apply this simple illustration to the role you will fill as head of your house. First, you must be open to communication from every member of your family—every need, every hurt, every pressure, every creative or constructive idea. Second, you must be able to assimilate all this information and decide on the appropriate action for the entire family to take. Although you receive input from each individual member, your decision must be what is best for the family as a whole. Third, having made your decision, you must initiate the action by the members of the family required to carry it out.

What will this require of you? First of all, sensitivity—the capacity to register the needs and feelings of others, to foresee problems and dangers, to accept and apply constructive ideas. Second, it will require the wisdom to make decisions that affect not only your own life, but also the lives of others. Third, it will require the strength of character and purpose to see that your decisions are carried out, enlisting where necessary the cooperation of others.

In 1 Timothy 3:4–5, Paul compares the responsibility of a church elder to that of a husband and father in his home: "He must manage his own family well and see that his children obey him with proper respect. (If anyone does not know how to manage his own family, how can he take care of God's church?)" The meaning of the verb translated *to manage* is to "stand at the head of or in front of." This is the position of the husband and father. He goes ahead of his family; he leads the way. Also, when evil or danger threatens his family, he stands in front of them, placing himself between them and what threatens them. All this can be summed up in one vital word: *leadership*.

In almost every section of society today, there is a dearth of effective leadership. There are also evil forces—both natural and supernatural—that oppose such leadership and seek to undermine it wherever it may arise. One major consequence has been the fearful disintegration of family life. God's plan for marriage and the home depends on the restoration of the kind of leadership the Bible depicts.

If you determine to be that kind of leader in your home, you must arm yourself beforehand to face opposition. You will be swimming against the current of contemporary culture. But after all, that is the difference between a live fish and a dead one: a live fish can swim against the current; a dead one can only float with it.

There are two foundations on which this kind of leadership must be based: responsibility and faithfulness. Normally, these are first acquired in seemingly humble or unimportant functions. Once acquired, they can provide the basis for success in any area of life. Without them, no real success is ever possible. Jesus said, "He who is faithful in a very little thing is faithful also in much; and he who is unrighteous in a very little thing is unrighteous also in much" (Luke 16:10, NASB).

I am reminded of a young man I knew—let's call him Arthur—who plunged deep into the drug culture. Then, miraculously, he met Jesus and was delivered from his addictions. But the powers of his mind and will had been eroded almost completely by the drugs. A pastor invited Arthur to live in his home and began the task of rehabilitation. The emphasis of his instruction was simple: In everything you are asked to do, seek the help of Jesus and be faithful.

After about two years, Arthur was given a job with a business firm. His responsibilities were the simplest and the most menial: sweeping the floor, emptying the trash, and so on. To all of them Arthur applied his mentor's formula: Seek the help of Jesus and be faithful. Gradually his faithfulness brought him promotions, each position more responsible than the one before. He was becoming a normal member of society once again.

After several more years with the firm, Arthur decided he needed to leave and get training in a more specialized vocation. When he began to explain to his employer what he proposed, the employer cut him short. "You can't leave! You're the only person in this firm I can trust. Stay with me and I'll train you to take over the business when I retire." Arthur was reaping the harvest he had sown by his persistent faithfulness.

Solomon's observations on faithfulness are very illuminating. In Proverbs 28:20 he says, "A faithful man will be richly blessed," while in Proverbs 20:6 he asks, "A faithful man who can find?" In the administration of his own great kingdom, Solomon acknowledged his need of faithful men. Yet, even with all the best men of Israel at his disposal, he had to search for one who fulfilled this qualification.

The twin characteristics of responsibility and faithfulness can be cultivated in almost any situation. Joseph cultivated them first in Potiphar's house, then in prison. The result was promotion. It nearly always will be!

People ask me where I received my training for the ministry. Sometimes I answer, "As a medical orderly with the British Army in North Africa." I had had academic training before I knew the Lord. In fact, I was overbalanced intellectually. What I needed was experience in confronting tough, real-life situations and accepting responsibility for the needs of others.

For a full year in the desert, I was leader of what the British Army called a "squad" of eight stretcher-bearers. Our home was a three-ton truck, which we shared with its two drivers. The eleven of us—living, eating, sleeping, and sharing hardship together—came to be known as "Prince's Pioneers."

During all this period, I had one constant companion: my Bible. I carried a pocket edition everywhere. Whenever I was not otherwise occupied, I was reading it. I was amazed to discover how practical it was. Again and again, it described a situation in which I found myself or a problem that confronted me. Always, too, it showed me God's answer. By the end of my time in the desert, I had a good, overall knowledge of the Bible, which has provided a solid foundation for every subsequent phase of my spiritual development.

For five years in the army, after I came to know the Lord, I maintained a consistent Christian testimony. On matters of conscience, I sometimes took a stand that brought me into confrontation with my fellow soldiers and with the officers over me. When I eventually received my discharge, the character rating recorded in my documents was the highest that the British Army awards: *Exemplary.* That was probably more significant than any theological diploma I could ever have earned.

Obviously, your life will not follow exactly the same pattern as mine. God deals with us all as individuals. Thank God He does! Neither the Church nor the world needs mass-produced Christians. On the other hand, there are certain general principles that apply to most of us.

First of all, commit yourself unreservedly to God (I dealt with this fully in chapter 4.) Then you can trust Him to guide you in the path that will fulfill His special plan for your life. A verse I have continually proven in my experience is Proverbs 3:6: "In all your ways acknowledge him, and he will make your paths straight."

Second, view every situation in which you find yourself as specially arranged by God to train you and develop some aspect of your character or personality. You may find yourself in some unexpected or unpleasant situations, but do not complain. Remember Joseph in the prison! I cannot say that I enjoyed most of my time in the desert, but I thank God for the way it equipped me for what lay ahead.

Third, make the Bible your first priority for study. Never let anything else take precedence over it. Seek to interpret every phase of your experience in the light of the Bible. You will be astonished at how much light it provides.

In the area of education, I recommend that you seek to relate all your studies to the course of life you believe God has appointed for you. Personally, I am not in favor of education for the sake of education. The "eternal student" is often a pathetic figure. Concerning this kind of life, the world's wisest man commented: "Of making many books there is no end, and much study wearies the body" (Ecclesiastes 12:12). Sometimes it seems there is no end to the obtaining of degrees, either!

Your spiritual development should normally find its full expression in the ordered life of fellowship provided by a local church. Here, under proper pastoral guidance, you will experience ongoing development in three related areas: your understanding of God's Word; your training for God's service; and the refining and strengthening of your Christian character. The same process that makes you a man of God "thoroughly equipped for every good work" (2 Timothy 3:17) will also prepare you for the headship of your home.

8

A Woman Prepares for Marriage

From Ruth's Perspective

How can I get ready for marriage? . . . I don't know if anybody will ever ask me! . . . I don't know what kind of man I might marry. . . . Every relationship I have ever had has failed. . . . There are no single Christian men who meet my expectations. . . . Getting married is a risk. I don't see that many good marriages, even in the Church. . . . Is it worthwhile to try to prepare when it may never happen anyway? . . . I don't want to waste my life waiting and wondering. . . .

Single women have said all these things to me. Every objection is valid. Today's young women face circumstances and problems unique to this century. From the time of Eve until our times, woman's destiny was settled: Either she would marry and rear children or, if no one claimed her, she would stay in the extended family and help those who needed her. This has changed drastically within living memory, particularly since the "liberation" of women.

There can be no question that women's liberation has brought many benefits. Countless women have been released

94

from exploitation or bondage that, in some cases, could be classified as slavery. Unfortunately, the balance sheet shows as many liabilities as assets. The divorce rate has skyrocketed; the marriage rate has declined; millions of babies have been aborted; other babies are unwanted and unloved; family life has deteriorated; multitudes of women are dissatisfied and unfulfilled.

In the face of all this, it is difficult for the young woman of today to know how to prepare for marriage. In previous generations, mothers and grandmothers trained their daughters as a normal part of daily living. But this is rare today. A woman whose own marriage has failed cannot teach her daughter by example. Often the mother herself had no training because *her* mother's marriage also failed. Furthermore, a woman who has worked hard all day to earn a living often has little time or energy to devote to teaching her daughter homemaking skills.

Part of the natural preparation for marriage is observing, within the family, the roles of each sex and the normal interrelationship between father and mother. The girl who grows up in a broken home cannot observe her mother in the role of wife. If she has no resident father, she is deprived of the opportunity to relate in a close and natural way to a man. A girl needs the admiration of her father as she begins to take steps toward maturity, both for her own self-esteem and to prepare her to relate to her husband.

Rather than receiving practical preparation for marriage, a girl of this generation is bombarded with humanist and feminist philosophies in the schools she attends, the movies she sees, the television she watches, the magazines she reads. She is taught how to make herself attractive. She is expected to prepare for a career and offered abundant opportunities for training—but not in how to succeed as a wife.

We may well ask: Is it even possible for a young woman to

be prepared for marriage today? In a society that has changed so much, is it worthwhile to even try to prepare? Shouldn't she just take her chances?

My answer is: For those willing to spend the time and effort, willing to "pay the price," preparation for marriage will bring uncounted rewards. Whether or not a woman ultimately marries, preparation for marriage can enable her to find fulfillment in life.

Furthermore, the effects are not limited to life on this earth. God has had a plan from before the beginnings of time to prepare a bride for His Son, the Lord Jesus. The Bible gives a vivid picture of the culmination of this age: the marriage supper of the Lamb.

Years before I anticipated marriage to Derek, I was challenged and inspired by the closing statement in Revelation 19:7: "And his bride has made herself ready." The Lord had revealed Himself to me when I was a forty-year-old divorced woman and filled me with incredible love for Himself. I marveled that He could love me so much, that He accepted me just as I was, that He had a specific plan for my life.

In this Scripture, however, I saw that His plan was not just to give me some temporary happiness. He wanted to share eternity with me! My responsibility was to make myself ready to be part of His bride.

This gave me a totally new perspective on my single state. Developing my character and learning to live a rewarding, satisfying life were not ends in themselves, but the pathway to something infinitely greater. From that time on, I found total fulfillment in serving my beloved Lord with all my heart.

A few years later, amazingly, unexpectedly, He brought Derek into my life, and soon I found myself preparing to marry my earthly bridegroom. (I share that story in Chapter 12.) What I discovered then, and continue to discover, is that the same qualities that make a woman pleasing to the Lord will make her pleasing to her mate.

If you will approach preparation for marriage at the earthly level with your heart turned toward the Lord Jesus, remembering that your ultimate destiny is to be part of His beautiful bride, then what you gain will be not only temporal happiness, but eternal bliss. Preparation for marriage will also prepare you for Jesus.

My primary purpose in this chapter, directed specifically toward women, is to help you to see your goal more clearly, and to direct you toward becoming the kind of woman who will complete—make whole—the man for whom God created you. I will offer proven, practical suggestions, taken from Scripture, from my own experience, and from other women.

These suggestions should improve the quality of your life as a single woman, whether you are still in school, living at home, or on your own holding down a job. They can be applied to your situation whether you are single, widowed, or divorced; whether you are 14 or 54. The qualities of character are ageless.

In my own case, I was actively pursuing a career and raising children when I began my preparation. Later I was a full-time servant of the Lord in Jerusalem, but the same principles applied. I hope my suggestions will stimulate you to seek ways to build your own character and enhance your own personality, in a manner uniquely appropriate for you. My twelve suggestions are by no means exhaustive!

First of all, let us consider how God views woman. Before He created her, He described her: "I will make a *helper* suitable for [man]" (Genesis 2:18, italics added). A woman's nature finds expression and fulfillment in helping.

Throughout the Bible God continues to fill out His picture of woman. I have compiled a list of twenty-six "Characteristics of a Helper" from my own study notes. Many women think that the Bible is a man's book, about men and for men. But I find it filled with practical direction and inspiration for every person, for every aspect of life.

Characteristics of a Helper

General	Home	Feminine
Wise	Industrious	Modest
Kind	Prudent	Pure
Faithful	Strong	Of meek & quiet
Loyal	Caring (for home	spirit
Sober	and family)	Priceless
Honorable	Capable	Trusting
Trustworthy	Dutiful	
Gracious		**Spiritual**
Courageous		Prayerful
Generous		Prophetic
		Ministering
		Devout
		Fearing the Lord

It is interesting to note that only six of these twenty-six characteristics relate specifically to the home, and only one (caring for the home and family) is *limited* to the home. In other words, you can develop them before you have your own home, and apply them whether you become a housewife or a working wife.

Ask the Holy Spirit to show you which of these qualities are most important for you at this time, and begin to seek ways to work them into your character.

Here, now, are my twelve suggestions:

1. Prepare to be a helper. When God created woman, He had a definite purpose in mind. He made her different from man because she has a different function. Not less important, but different. He made woman to be "a helper suitable for [man]" (Genesis 2:18). Some of the major problems of the twentieth century, it seems to me, relate directly to frustrated womanhood. Millions of women are unable to fulfill the purpose for which they were created.

I can testify to this firsthand. As a career woman, I was quite successful. Both before and after I earned my college degree, every job change I made was a promotion. I was a private secretary, an office manager, a classroom teacher, an executive assistant, and an administrator for the State of Maryland responsible for a $2 million annual budget. But I was never fully content. Only when I married Derek did I find the deep satisfaction that comes from being the helper God created me to be.

Looking back, however, it has become clear to me that I needed *all* that experience to be Derek's helper. Those were not wasted years. They were years of preparation.

If you are to be a successful wife, you must face up to the fact that God has not changed His standards or His intentions. You must decide in your heart that you want to be what God created you to be. Only then can you begin to consider how to achieve it. You do not begin by finding a mate; you begin with yourself.

Until you are married, you cannot know the exact kind of helper you will need to be. Your husband's vocation and temperament will determine that. Normally, however, the primary way a wife helps her husband is by making a home for him. This is true regardless of her husband's vocation, and whether or not she is a working wife.

It is generally the wife who markets, brings home the food, cooks it, and serves it. She does the laundry and keeps the home clean. She is responsible for decorating it appropriately. During the years the children are small, much of her activity centers in the home. The woman has the responsibility to God and to her husband to mold and shape the characters of the little lives that are entrusted to them.

It is from his home that the husband goes out to the world, to succeed or fail, to be fulfilled or frustrated. The wife who creates an atmosphere of love and encouragement, of peace and stability, can expect to share in the blessings and rewards of her husband's successes.

Whether homemaking is interesting and challenging or dull and dreary is determined by her attitude. Modern appliances and kitchen equipment can either "liberate" her from the home or challenge her to new heights of creativity. If you will prepare your attitude now, and view your future home as the means of expressing your love and gratitude toward God and your husband, you will have taken the first step toward being a happy, successful, fulfilled wife. The other facets of your role as helper will develop as you learn to function with your husband as a team.

The wife who is pursuing her own career, or who is holding down a job in order to help support the family, will always find herself in a state of tension between her primary role of helper and this secondary role. Juggling the two roles is a never-ending challenge. The most significant advice I can offer is that you see your priorities clearly and do all in your power to keep your primary role in first place.

The wife in Proverbs 31:10–31 provides an example of a woman who has embraced the vision of being a helper. Here is a businesswoman who manages the family affairs so successfully that her husband is freed to take his place of leadership in the city. She buys and sells. She extends generous hands to the poor. She speaks with wisdom. And her husband "has full confidence in her" (verse 11).

2. Cultivate your relationship with the Lord. Your heavenly Father has a plan for your life that is "good, and acceptable, and perfect" (Romans 12:2, KJV). You can move more quickly into that plan by deliberately choosing to get close to God and to hear what He is saying to you *personally* day by day. If you do not already have a rich relationship with the Lord, you need to learn how to draw near to Him in your daily quiet time.

I want to emphasize that there is no exact pattern that works for everyone. We are all different; we each relate to God according to our own personalities. But I would like to share very personally from my own experience during the years before I married Derek. Perhaps one or more of my examples will be just what you need to point you in the right direction.

I am assuming you have already experienced the new birth, and that you have made a full, unreserved commitment of your life to the Lord. If you have not already taken this first vital step, and you really want to be prepared for your mate, may I suggest that you pause before reading any further in this chapter and turn back to the fourth chapter, "The Gateway."

Here now are seven specific suggestions:

a. *Remember that relationships take time.* We must be willing to spend time with the Lord, to worship Him, to read His Word, to pray, to wait upon Him. Without this, we can never fully develop. There are too many "retarded Christians"— precious souls who came to new life with all the resources of the Godhead available to them, but who have never disciplined themselves to partake of that wealth.

Bear in mind that no woman can give to her husband any more than she has within her. A woman's full beauty and potential will never be realized if she is underdeveloped or undeveloped spiritually. Now is the time to lay a solid foundation on which to build throughout a lifetime, whether single or married.

b. *Give God your best time.* For most of us, this is early in the morning before we face the world. Single women can learn to focus on Jesus, our heavenly Bridegroom. Once we see Him in that way, we can do nothing less than make the expression of our love for Him our highest priority. Almost from the day I met Jesus in 1970, I have made it a practice each day not to speak to anyone else until I have spoken with the Lord. He helps me to prepare for the day. Even when I had to leave home for my work at 7:30 a.m., I rose at five so I wouldn't cheat the Lord.

c. *Begin with thanksgiving and praise.* I begin each day by thanking Him for loving me, for the blood of Jesus, for the beauty of creation, for the privilege of serving Him. I turn my face to Him, open my mouth and sing. He says:

> Show me your face,
> let me hear your voice;
> for your voice is sweet,
> and your face is lovely.
> (Song of Songs 2:14)

Ours is a very personal relationship. I am not a great singer, but it pleases the Lord when I sing to Him. I memorize songs from worship cassettes. I used to carry a tiny hymnbook to the bathroom and memorize old hymns while brushing my teeth and putting on makeup. I have a varied repertoire, available as the Holy Spirit leads.

d. *Read your Bible before you pray.* We honor God by allowing Him to speak to us before we begin to speak to Him. I have profited by keeping markers in two places, reading from the New Testament in the morning and the Old Testament at night. For a period I read a portion every day from the historical books, the Psalms and prophets, and the New Testament (for which I needed three markers).

e. *Keep a prayer list, especially if you pray alone.* This helped me personally to focus my mind and stay on target. I made a simple list of names and situations, grouped by category—for example, for salvation, for healing, for direction, for spiritual leaders, for specific segments of the Church, for nations. One important pointer: Don't give all your prayer time to problem people. Pray also for those making an impact for the Kingdom of God. Derek and I rely on the daily prayers of others in the Body of Christ; we bless them each day in our private prayers.

When I prayed alone, I also kept a simple notebook of Scriptures that spoke to me at special times, and of prophetic words from the Lord. During a down day, and during the long months I was a semi-invalid, these were a constant source of encouragement. Another thing: Don't hesitate to pray for yourself. Don't get bogged down in your own problems, but do ask God to help you to overcome in problem areas. He is ready to hear and answer because He wants to make us over in the image of His Son.

f. *Don't limit the Lord to quiet times.* I relate to the Lord continually—I always have the conversational lines open. When I was alone, I had Scripture or Bible teaching cassettes always available so that I was never lonely. In spare moments I filled my mind with portions of Scripture or read from devotional material. I learned especially to communicate with the Lord when my hands were busy but my mind was comparatively free—washing dishes, ironing, personal grooming, driving the car. All these habits established in my single life have enriched (and continue to enrich) my married life.

g. *Check on yourself to make sure God is in first place.* God hates lukewarmness. "Because you are lukewarm—neither hot nor cold—I am about to spit you out of my mouth" (Revelation 3:16). Someone has said, "If you were ever closer to Jesus than you are today, you are backslidden." People backslide in tiny, almost imperceptible steps. Check on yourself before that happens. It is a long, hard road back, and few ever make it. Don't lose what you have!

3. Cultivate commitment and loyalty. You cannot begin to practice commitment and loyalty the day you get married. If you have not first given yourself wholeheartedly to the Lord, and then to some person or cause, you will not be prepared to give yourself to your husband.

If you are employed, are you committed to your employer? Or are you a hireling who counts the hours and looks for excuses for time off? If you live at home, do you take responsibility for your tasks, or do you always have to be reminded? Are you loyal to your family? When you make a promise, do you keep it, or do you find an excuse to renege?

Are you committed to your church or prayer group? Can you be depended on to carry through on projects for which you have volunteered?

Read the Parable of the Sower in Matthew 13 and make up your mind to be soil in which good seed will bring forth a good harvest.

4. Cultivate your own self-esteem. Many women marry the wrong man or fail in their marriages because they do not set a high enough value on themselves. You are a child of God. Jesus valued you so highly and loved you so much that He died for you! The New Testament and Psalms are filled with Scriptures that encourage believers to see themselves as God sees them. Spend some time memorizing them, to have them instantly available. Here are a few:

But we all, with open face beholding as in a glass the glory of the Lord, are changed into the same image from glory to glory, even as by the Spirit of the Lord.

(2 Corinthians 3:18, KJV)

For in him dwelleth all the fulness of the Godhead bodily. And ye are complete in him, which is the head of all principality and power.

(Colossians 2:9–10, KJV)

For it is God which worketh in you both to will and to do of his good pleasure.

(Philippians 2:13, KJV)

For we are his workmanship, created in Christ Jesus unto good works, which God hath before ordained that we should walk in them.

(Ephesians 2:10, KJV)

Satan's primary activity against believers is accusation. Another is discouragement. Our best answer, just as it was for Jesus, is the Word of God. As you read and pray, the Holy Spirit may show you areas in which you need to change or improve. Do not yield to condemnation or self-pity when that happens. Rather, ask the Lord to help you and exercise your own will to bring it about. If you need deliverance from evil spirits, or if there is a curse over your life that has never been broken, seek spiritual counseling. Whom the Son has set free is free indeed!

An important result of developing your self-esteem is that you will be better able to encourage and upbuild your husband. Thus you will be able to help him reach his own full potential. It is a rare man who can develop beyond the expectations of his wife. Her opinion of him is vital to his success.

The wife who sees all her husband's potential can encourage him, pray for him, and then have the excitement of watching God bring it to fulfillment.

5. Be willing to learn. Another look at the Proverbs 31 woman should encourage you to develop in as many areas as you can. If you are in school (either high school or college), be sure you also give time to practical skills: sewing, cooking and nutrition, child care, household management, home decorating, flower arranging, handcrafts, needlework. Let the Holy Spirit lead you into special areas: interpretive dance, music, photography, pottery making, woodworking. He knows exactly what you will need to be your husband's helper. (You may even meet your husband-to-be in one of these classes!) Don't underestimate the value of sports and physical fitness activities.

If you are already working and have never had the opportunity to acquire these practical skills, make it a priority. Check out your local adult education center, find a busy homemaker who would like to make you her apprentice/helper an evening or two a week, and use your initiative! If you procrastinate, you yourself may be the reason for delay in meeting your mate. God wants you prepared!

Since much of your responsibility will entail caring for your children, you need to learn as much as you can in advance. Most young women have the opportunity to babysit, but some courses in early childhood development and even adolescent psychology will supplement those practical skills.

Be diligent to avoid passive occupations that leave you empty and your senses dulled, especially television. You are a beautiful creation with God's life within you. You can never recover a lost day—or a lost hour. By all means relax, but relax in ways that will build you up. Use your time wisely now. As your responsibilities increase, your discretionary time will decrease. Now is your opportunity to invest your time in activities that will bring forth dividends throughout your life, whether single or married.

6. Be willing to serve. There is no better way for a woman to express her love for her husband than by serving him. How she serves him will depend on his personality and career, but the loving wife will study her husband and learn to anticipate his needs even before he asks. Keeping your home as an expression of your love for your husband and as a service to him will take away the drudgery.

How can you prepare beforehand to serve your husband? By serving others with gladness of heart! Derek and I have been blessed through the years of our marriage by a succession of young women who have served us in our home. I have watched them blossom as their confidence in their own abilities increased. The words of Jesus in Luke 16:10–12 are so appropriate for single women. If you are willing to serve others, to be faithful in the little things and over someone else's property, God will, in His time give you your own.

Don't limit yourself to the obvious areas of service— visiting the sick and doing volunteer work in a hospital or a church. These are important, but look also for ways you can enhance your skills at the same time.

Ask the Lord to show you those skills that will prepare you to be your husband's helper. They will certainly not be limited to homemaking. One of the happiest wives I know rejoiced when she could become her husband's bookkeeper as he started his own business, since she already had the training. Another, a pastor's wife, designs and clothes herself and their family of girls. With her skilled fingers, she can copy ideas she sees in expensive designer shops. Her husband reaps the compliments for his beautiful home and family, and blesses them in return.

A few years ago Derek and I undertook the building of a home in Jerusalem. We have a very active, busy life in ministry, and I chafed at the time and energy it took to plan, purchase, and coordinate the furnishing of a home from 6,000 miles away. I had acquired the necessary skills years before, but I considered them less important than some other things. My attitude was changed by a single sentence from Derek: "Perhaps this is part of your preparation for eternity; perhaps the Lord will want you to furnish a galaxy in eternity!" Now, as we enjoy our home, I thank God continually that I had the privilege of making it a beautiful, peaceful sanctuary where we can pray and write. When you begin to view your own service as preparation for eternity, your whole perspective changes!

In daily life, practice treating others as you like to be treated. Much of the art of serving is just old-fashioned good manners—being considerate and thoughtful of others. Some of the most loving young women and men I have met are those who were trained as waiters and waitresses.

I can honestly say the task that satisfies me most is serving Derek. Even before we married, I began to look for ways to lift burdens from him. Since our marriage, I have learned to take responsibility for all the practical details of daily living. I try to keep life as uncomplicated for him as possible, whether we are at home or on ministry journeys. When traveling, I carry in my suitcase a variety of gadgets and provisions to make Derek as comfortable as possible in every situation.

We still chuckle whenever we recall an incident in London's

airport a few years ago. We were en route to Belfast, so a thorough search was made of all our luggage. The security officer shook his head in amazement at my doorstop (we have had a few experiences where a host's child burst into our room unannounced) and my bathtub stopper (at least one in four hotel rooms has an ineffective bathtub stopper).

When the officer came to my teapot with cozy, he became more and more interested in us. I explained that outside the United Kingdom, most hotels do not provide tea-making facilities in the rooms, and I always carried this so that I could provide early morning tea for my husband.

Finally the officer opened little gingham bags containing dried fruit and nuts and asked, "Lady, why do you carry this?" I explained that sometimes room service in hotels was not available, and I always tried to have something on hand in case my husband was hungry. He closed my suitcase, looked at me, and said, "You are the best prepared lady I have ever seen!"

I endeavor to be diligent to do only those things for Derek that no one else can do. The rest I delegate. If I become too busy with too many details, I cannot be flexible enough to be available to him at a moment's notice. One of my main responsibilities is to protect him from unnecessary interruptions and from people who make unreasonable demands on his time.

7. **Be willing to adjust to your husband's priorities.** The Living Bible speaks of "saintly women of old, who trusted God and fitted in with their husbands' plans" (1 Peter 3:5). It is the wife's duty to be flexible, ready to adapt to her husband's desires because he is the head (1 Corinthians 11:3). He sets the pattern for the way their lives will flow together. The wife should be queen in the home, but the husband is king!

I admire Rebecca, who left her home, family, and culture to go with a servant into an unknown future and to marry a man she had not yet met. She demonstrated faith and adaptability. I also admire Sarah, who left the security of Ur to travel around with her husband for most of her life. Bearing a child at 90 must have required a major change in her lifestyle!

Flexibility is needed not only for big moves, but in the little things of daily life. I was a morning person, Derek is a night person. But by the grace of God, I have changed so that we both keep the same schedule. I have also learned to nap with him in the afternoon; thus we really have two days every day.

In my case, too, we have three lifestyles—one in our home in Jerusalem, where we live quietly, spending much time in intercession and writing; one in Florida, where we are involved with the many activities of Derek Prince Ministries and the church where Derek is an elder; and another when we travel several months of each year in ministry. I thank God every day that I learned to be flexible before I married Derek! It would have been too late if I had waited until afterward to learn.

I have watched some young women change their hair and clothing styles, the way they cook, and the way they entertain, as they have adjusted to their husband's desires. Pleasing your husband will bring you many more blessings than pleasing yourself.

8. Learn to pray and intercede for others. "And pray in the Spirit on all occasions with all kinds of prayers and requests. . . . Be alert and always keep on praying for all the saints. Pray also for me. . . ." (Ephesians 6:18–19).

God is looking for intercessors. As you spend time with the Lord daily, ask Him to show you what is on *His* heart that you can pray about. As you learn to intercede, there will be no shortage of topics. God will bring people and situations to your mind. And people will ask for your prayers.

There are two fringe benefits for single women who are intercessors. First, it takes their minds off themselves, their problems, and their single state (if this for them poses a problem). Second, it prepares them to intercede for their husbands. Two young women I know, whose husbands were good but not extraordinary men, began to pray and intercede for their husbands two or three hours every day. Two years later, both men are outstandingly successful, prospering spiritually and prospering in their careers. Much of your husband's success will depend on your ability to intercede.

Ask God to bring you together with another likeminded single woman for prayer. "Again I say unto you, That if two of you shall agree on earth as touching any thing that they shall ask, it shall be done for them of my Father which is in heaven" (Matthew 18:19, KJV). Learning to pray with a partner will prepare you to pray in harmony with your husband.

I owe a great debt to two dear Dutch sisters in Jerusalem who intercede together in wonderful harmony. One day as they visited me during my months of invalidism, they prayed spontaneously that God would give me a prayer partner. A little more than a year later I was married to Derek. Their prayer was answered in a way none of us expected!

9. Learn proper care of your body. Most young women take their bodies for granted. Unless they have had some major medical problem, they have ample strength for life's demands. I was 32 when my mother-in-law admonished me, "You must learn to conserve your strength. You won't always have it." I laughed. I was so strong. Six years later I wished I had listened. With every decade it gets more difficult to restore one's strength. God has done several miracles for me since 1968, but I still have to give diligent attention to nutrition and exercise to meet the demands of my calling in God.

God spoke to Derek more than twenty years ago: "If you are to fulfill the ministry I have for you, you will need a strong, healthy body, and you are putting on too much weight." Not everyone gets such personal direction, but it is no less apt for you and me. We need strong, healthy bodies to fulfill God's plan for our lives.

Today we know it is not loving to give our husbands and children candy and rich desserts—or even big juicy steaks. In the last fifteen years there has been a tremendous move toward natural foods and away from white sugar, white flour, red meats, and fats. Many middle-aged men and women who have suffered heart attacks or major cardiovascular problems are finding help in diet and exercise.

Younger people can benefit from all that has been learned and thus avoid the mistakes and illnesses of previous generations. The American Institute for Cancer Research reports that cancer can often be prevented by proper diet and use of certain vitamins and minerals.

Feeding the family and developing good food habits is the wife's responsibility. The more you can learn before you marry, and the more appealing recipes you have already perfected, the more ready you will be to keep your husband and children well and strong.

Now is also the time to develop your body through physical exercise and sports. One of the best ways to overcome boredom and frustration is physical activity. Later you will find that participating in sports together is one of the most satisfying ways a husband and wife can relax together. Prepare yourself now by developing a variety of skills in sports: swimming, skiing, windsurfing, snorkeling, jogging, racquetball, tennis.

At our ages, Derek and I find walking and hiking our best physical activities. Walking hand-in-hand as we do is a real secret to maintaining harmony, both physical and spiritual.

"Can two walk together, except they be agreed?" (Amos 3:3, KJV).

There are many good books on nutrition and fitness. I will mention just two: *Aerobics for Women* by Betty Cooper and *The Pritikin Program for Diet and Exercise* by Nathan Pritikin. An extra benefit: Physically fit, properly nourished young women have much easier pregnancies and labor, and have healthier babies.

10. Observe the wife's behavior in exemplary marriages. One of my first discoveries as a new believer was that certain Christian women had a different attitude toward their husbands than I had ever seen. I was impressed and challenged by their femininity and their devotion to their husbands. They seemed entirely satisfied in their roles and fulfilled in their ways of life.

Even though I had no thoughts at that time that I would marry again, I could not help observing their behavior. I saw then that I needed the same qualities I saw in them to prepare me for Jesus, my Bridegroom.

Look around at the married women you know. Ask the Holy Spirit to show you the qualities suitable for you (and the things to avoid!). Don't try to be a carbon copy of anyone. If you have a lively personality, you can acquire a meek and quiet spirit without becoming a mouse. Some naturally quiet women are just plain dull—or they may be quietly bitter and sharp-tongued. A meek and quiet spirit is an *attitude*.

Bear in mind, too, that someday you may be someone's role model, if you are diligent to prepare yourself and continue your development after marriage. You want to be able to say, "Be imitators of me, just as I also am of Christ" (1 Corinthians 11:1, NASB).

11. Trust God. Be willing to wait. Derek has already spoken about this in chapter 6, "Eight Guidelines To

Follow." I mention it again, however, because trusting is one of the particularly feminine traits listed at the beginning of this chapter. God loves you. "No good thing will he withhold from them that walk uprightly" (Psalm 84:11, KJV). Providing you meet His conditions, He will care for you whether you are single or married.

Too often women enter into a marriage because they fear they will never have another chance. Then they learn it was better to be single than to be married to the wrong man. Their lives become shipwrecked, and often the lives of their children and grandchildren as well.

I know women, on the other hand, who have gone on to find fulfillment in their personal lives and careers until God brought them to their perfect mates. One dear friend was 39 when she married; I met her when she was 69, a perfect wife to her husband. Another, a divorcee, was alone twenty-one years; then, at age 58, she met a widower. Seldom have I seen a more perfect match! Each of these women would have missed God's best if she had married the wrong man or settled totally into single life. God kept his hand on them because they trusted in Him.

12. Set your goals; establish your priorities. Your goals and priorities will not be exactly the same as mine. God was preparing me to marry Derek. He may be preparing you to be the perfect helper for someone who is quite different. You must set your own personal goals. But regardless of the goals, the same principles apply.

Go back to page 96 and read through "Characteristics of a Helper"; then review points 1–11 above. Ask the Lord to help you find the ones that are appropriate for you, areas where you are falling short, or traits you have never before considered. Make a list first of these long-term goals.

From that list, choose several short-term goals that you

could reasonably attain in the next three months, six months, or the next year. Be realistic. Consider your present abilities. Don't aim to run in a marathon next week if you have never jogged further than from the refrigerator to the TV. Consider your present responsibilities—your study or your work, an aged parent for whom you are responsible, or children from a previous marriage. If you have been ill or have neglected your health and nutrition, you should give care of your body a high priority.

After you set your goals, you can establish the priorities that will lead you to them. Don't try to do everything at once. On the other hand, the Holy Spirit may lead you to work on more than one area at a time.

One thing that might help is keeping a record of how you use your time. Be honest. Then go over it and decide what is most important (1, 2, 3, etc.). Begin to bring your use of time in line with the degree of importance of each activity. Fit your new goals in their appropriate places. As you shift your priorities, your life will begin to change.

When I did this a number of years ago, two of the first things to drop off my list were idle conversation (even though it was about spiritual things) and fruitless counseling sessions. I had often spent hours counseling people who would not meet the conditions for spiritual growth.

We are responsible to God for how we use our time, and for every idle word spoken. I don't want to stand before God and have Him say, "You could have done better."

9

The Role of
Parents and Pastors

It is natural for parents to be concerned about the mates their children marry. In different cultures and periods of history, parents have expressed this concern in a variety of ways. In some forms of Judaism, the choice of mates was at one time the exclusive responsibility of the parents. This is still true among various Arab and Asiatic peoples today.

To most people in our Western culture, such a practice seems medieval and ridiculously autocratic. But before accepting such a judgment, we should take time to evaluate the results. On *this* basis, Western culture cannot afford to point a finger at any other system. No other culture in human history has produced so high a proportion of unhappy and broken marriages, with all their inevitable train of evil social consequences.

Is there one specific system for arranging marriages that is superior to all the others? I would be inclined to answer no. There are, however, certain principles that always apply. These can be made to work successfully in various cultures and social systems. Parents may follow these principles on behalf of their children, or children may apply them to their own lives. In either case, the results will depend on the principles that are applied rather than on the persons who apply them.

The basis for success may be summed up in one word: respect. This has three different aspects: respect for God and His Word; respect for marriage; and respect for human personality. I have dealt with each of these aspects in previous chapters of this book. Where respect of this kind is supplanted by wrong attitudes and motives—such as lust, covetousness, pride, or selfish ambition—there is no system that can produce a successful marriage.

The Bible record indicates a considerable degree of flexibility in the way some of its main characters entered into marriage. Abraham, for instance, accepted responsibility for obtaining a bride for his son Isaac, and sent his servant back to Mesopotamia for this purpose. The servant was given certain stipulations in his choice, but in the last resort he depended on prayer to reveal the woman God had chosen (see Genesis 24:12–14). This accords fully with the principles set forth earlier in this book.

Isaac's two sons, Esau and Jacob, both made their own choice of mates, Esau contrary to the desires of his parents. Jacob followed his parents' directions, but actually made his own choice and negotiated the terms of his two marriages with his uncle Laban. It is significant that the son who accepted his parents' directions was more successful than the one who did not.

In the period of the Judges, Samson made his own choice of a Philistine wife, contrary to his parents' desires. Samson persuaded his parents, however, to make the actual matrimonial arrangements on his behalf. In his choice of a wife, Samson went against both the Law of Moses and his parents' counsel. This set him on a course that led to his ultimate disaster.

Irrespective of any particular system of arranging marriages, it is clear that parents have both a deep concern and an important responsibility to see that their children make successful marriages. In our contemporary culture, how should parents set about achieving this goal? The following are five specific ways parents can contribute to the success of their children's marriages.

1. Prayer. The day to start praying for God's appointed mates for your children is the day each one of them is born. This kind of prayer is a long-term investment, but it pays tremendous dividends. It is so much better to pray this through in advance than to wait until some crisis threatens, and then to start praying prayers of desperation. Often these can prove no more successful than locking the stable door after the horse has bolted.

One couple I know began to pray for mates for each of their children as soon as they were born. Today, more than thirty years later, all five of their children are committed Christians with mates likewise committed. Furthermore, the pathway to their marriages was not marked by many of the pressures and traumas many young people go through today.

2. Example. If you want your children to seek God's best in marriage, set them a visible standard to aim at. There is no more effective way than by your example. Merely offering them rules that they never see put into practice is more likely to produce a negative result than a positive one. It is a tragic fact that many young people today have never seen a happy marriage. Consequently, they approach marriage with cynicism and disillusionment. Any marriage that develops out of these attitudes is almost doomed to failure even before the vows have been pronounced.

In talking with young people facing problems, and in observing marriages that are successful, I have concluded there is one element in the home that children long for more than any other, though they themselves may not be conscious of it. It is *harmony*. If harmony begins with the parents, it will normally flow from them into the character and conduct of the children. But if the parents cannot achieve harmony between themselves, there is little hope for the children.

An atmosphere of harmony in the home does more to meet children's needs than many of the material benefits that today are considered almost indispensable. During the years I pastored in London, Lydia and I often lived on a meager budget. I can remember buying my razor blades one at a time because I could not afford a whole packet! Many years later, I asked one of our daughters what her impressions were of that period when we were poor. She looked at me in surprise. "I never thought of you and Mummy as being poor!" she said.

There is another benefit of harmony between parents: it enables them to pray for their children the kinds of prayers God is committed to answering. His promise is contained in Matthew 18:19: "Again, I tell you that if two of you on earth agree [literally, *harmonize*] about anything you ask for, it will be done for you by my Father in heaven."

3. Training. In Ephesians 6:4 (already quoted in chapter 7), God places on the father in each home the responsibility for training the children in the ways of God: "Fathers, do not exasperate your children; instead, bring them up in the training and instruction of the Lord."

I do not take this verse to mean that the father must bear this responsibility alone and that the mother has no part in it. The father does have the primary responsibility to initiate the process of training the children and setting the overall patterns and goals. But within this framework, the mother has a vitally important contribution to make. After all, in most families today, she is the one who spends the most time with the children—especially when they are young and impressionable. She has countless opportunities every day to confirm and enforce the principles established by the father. If she sees herself in the biblical role of helper, there is no area in which her help is more important than in the training of the children.

The main emphasis should be on training, not just on teaching. Teaching is communicating to children the truths they need to know. Training is seeing that they apply those truths in daily living. Children may receive teaching in various places—church, Sunday school, even secular school. But the home is the main place they should receive training.

In chapters 5 through 8, Ruth and I have explained various aspects of attitude and conduct that will enable a young person to find the right mate and to build a successful marriage. But none of these will suddenly appear by some happy coincidence in the life of a young person at the point he or she is confronted by the issue of marriage. Such aspects of attitude and conduct can be achieved only by years of careful training. Parents who provide their children with this kind of training are helping them lay the foundation for a lifetime of married happiness.

4. Fellowship. Training of this kind does not normally take place in a classroom situation. Nor is it accomplished by some carefully prepared lecture. A classroom or lecture situation is too theoretical. It tends to leave young people with the impression that what is being imparted is not related to the business of daily living. The kind of atmosphere needed is best provided by casual, ongoing fellowship in a situation that is neither "religious" nor "academic."

In Deuteronomy 6:7 Moses counsels parents in Israel how to transmit to their children the Lord's commandments: "Impress them on your children. Talk about them when you sit at home and when you walk along the road, when you lie down and when you get up." Almost identical counsel is repeated in Deuteronomy 11:19. The setting Moses recommends for this kind of instruction is the simple, daily activities of family life.

What would be some corresponding situations in our contemporary culture? A son helping his father mow the yard or carry out minor repairs on the family car. A mother in the kitchen with her daughter, showing her how to bake cookies, or in the living room removing a stain from the carpet. Other activities involving the whole family might be a camping vacation or a visit to a site important in the nation's history. Perhaps the most obvious place for fellowship and training is the meal table—one reason why it is important for families to eat together regularly.

In any or all of these situations, parents have unlimited opportunities to inculcate habits of good behavior, combined with practical work principles of orderliness and thoroughness. At the same time, they can interweave basic truths of God's Word in a way that brings out their relevance to the business of living.

Whatever the situation, there is one essential, unvarying requirement. It is *time*—time when parents are together with their children in a natural, relaxed atmosphere. Time invested wisely in children at their most impressionable stage of development will produce results that endure throughout the rest of their lives and on into eternity.

5. Counsel. As children pass through adolescence into adulthood, the need for ongoing fellowship with their parents continues, though it may become more intermittent due to the claims of education or employment. Young adults finding their own way through the world, setting their own lifestyles, making their own decisions, are probably less conscious of their need for their parents, though it may actually be greater.

At this stage, the opportunities for training will decrease. In its place, however, another need will arise: that of counsel. The transition from training to counsel requires a different attitude in parents. Training can be enforced; counsel can only be offered. (Parents often find it harder to make this transition than their children do!)

Much depends on the relationship parents have built with their children up to this point. If it is one of mutual love, confidence, and respect, then it is natural for children to turn to their parents for counsel when they face problems or important decisions. Sooner or later, the most critical decision they have to face will probably be the choice of a mate.

How can parents be ready to respond with appropriate counsel? First, they must be armed with a clear scriptural understanding of the divine plan for marriage. Only this can provide the strength and stability their children need.

When a child's plans harmonize with the divine pattern, the task of parents is simple: to offer ongoing guidance and encouragement. When a child is contemplating a marriage not in line with the principles of Scripture, on the other hand, parents must look to the Lord for a unique combination of grace and strength.

Grace will enable them to share the struggles and agonies that a young person passes through at such a time. Strength will enable them to continue upholding God's standard in the face of intense pressure to accept less than they know to be God's best for their child. The issue will probably be settled by their prayers and by the kind of spiritual foundation laid in the child's life through the preceding years.

The main responsibility for steering young people into successful marriage normally rests upon the parents. But when the members of the family attend a church, it is likely that the pastoral leadership will also become involved. What responsibility do pastors bear in such a situation? And how can they fulfill it?

First of all, pastors should be careful not to come between parents and their children. So long as parents are willing to accept responsibility for their children, the pastor's role should be to guide and strengthen the parents, but not to take over their function. The marriage or approaching marriage of one of the children sometimes causes powerful tensions within a family. Whenever possible, the family should handle these tensions together as a unit. This will strengthen the bonds between them for the years to come.

It may be, however, that the parents find themselves unable to handle the situation on their own, and turn to their pastor for help. If so, it is extremely important for pastor and parents to stand together. On the one hand, the parents should respect and follow the pastor's counsel, unless it contradicts their own deep convictions. On the other hand, the pastor should do everything in his power to honor and uphold the position of the parents in their family.

Parents and pastor, standing together in this way, may rescue a precious young life from a carefully planned snare of the devil. If the devil can insinuate disharmony and division between them, on the other hand, he may succeed in capturing a sheep from the Lord's fold.

Unfortunately, in this age of broken family relationships, many young people cannot look to their parents for effective guidance or instruction concerning marriage. Where shall they turn? First of all, to the Lord! He hears the cry of every soul who sincerely seeks Him.

Those who do turn to God and commit their lives to Him will probably be directed by Him to a place of Christian fellowship, under some kind of effective pastoral oversight. Here it will be natural for them to look to the pastoral leadership for the kind of guidance and instruction they should have received from their parents. A pastor may find himself assuming responsibility of a parental nature for young people who are not his natural children. He will thus be combining in himself the roles of pastor and parent.

Any servant of God willing to accept this responsibility is to be highly commended. He will experience unusual burdens, but also unusual blessings! Before he commits himself to such a position, however, he needs to be sure of two important points. First, that the parents have been given the opportunity to accept their responsibility and have proved either unable or unwilling. Second, that the young person has done everything possible to establish a right relationship with the parents. (I dealt with this issue in chapter 5 on right attitudes.)

One responsibility that rests on all pastors is to provide their people with thorough, scriptural instruction on marriage in all its aspects. This should cover the mutual responsibilities of both parents and children. It might be beneficial to conduct a special seminar each year for young people in the church who are passing from adolescence into adulthood, entitled something like "Face to Face with Marriage" or "How to Find Your Mate." I predict it would meet with an enthusiastic response. More than that, it could help to resolve many of the special problems young people are likely to encounter. Surely it is better to lock the stable door before the horse escapes!

This kind of ministry fits into the prophetic picture of the world situation as this present age draws to its close. In the closing verses of the Old Testament God makes this declaration:

> See, I will send you the prophet Elijah before that great and dreadful day of the Lord comes. He will turn the hearts of the fathers to their children, and the hearts of the children to their fathers; or else I will come and strike the land with a curse.
>
> (Malachi 4:5-6)

God confronts us here with three matters of extreme urgency. First, the critical social problem of this closing period will be strife between parents and children, resulting in broken homes. Second, unless this problem is resolved, it will bring God's curse on the land. And third, God will raise up a special ministry to provide His solution to the problem.

Surely it is the responsibility of the Church to be a part of this solution!

Special Situations

10

Divorce and Remarriage

Divorce is a major contemporary social problem. Its harmful effects extend far beyond the couple who obtain a divorce. If there are children, they almost invariably suffer great emotional strains. Often they are left with a warped, negative view of marriage and the family.

Beyond the individuals directly affected, however, divorce is a main lever used by the forces of evil to break up the life of the family and thus to endanger the whole fabric of society. Any culture or civilization that opens the way for promiscuous, uncontrolled divorce has forged an instrument for its own destruction. As surely as it has sown the wind, it will reap the whirlwind.

Tragically, divorce has become almost as common within the professing Christian Church as it is in the non-Christian world. In this area, too, the ultimate consequence must inevitably be the disintegration of the Church.

What has opened the way for divorce to become so prevalent among Christians? Two main causes may be adduced. The first is a wrong view of marriage, in which the

Church has abandoned the standards of God and of Scripture. In their place it has embraced those of the world. Someone has illustrated this by the following "parable": A ship in the sea is all right; the sea in a ship is all wrong. The Church in the world is all right; the world in the Church is all wrong.

The second main cause for the upsurge of divorce among Christians is that many have received, at best, inadequate preparation for marriage. They enter into marriage with no clear understanding of its nature or its obligations. Very often, too, they have not received the instruction and training that would enable them to fulfill those obligations. The result is like a couple at sea in a boat, neither of whom knows how to row or to steer.

It is my sincere desire and prayer that this book will provide a constructive solution for both these problems—the ignorance concerning the nature of marriage and the lack of preparation for it.

Over the centuries, the Church has frequently failed to face the problem of divorce in a realistic way, or has imposed regulations that are both unfair and unscriptural. One main reason has probably been the enforced celibacy of the clergy. Those responsible for making the regulations knew in advance that they themselves would never have to abide by them. Jesus might well have said of such men what He said of the Pharisees in His own day: "They tie up heavy loads and put them on men's shoulders, but they themselves are not willing to lift a finger to move them" (Matthew 23:4).

Like the Pharisees, church leaders devised ingenious ways to circumvent their own regulations when it suited them. For the wealthy or the influential, "annulment" produced the same practical results as divorce without infringing the letter of their law.

Certainly it was never God's intention for marriage to end in divorce. Traced to its source, divorce is always a result of man's departure from God's ways and standards. That is no justification, however, for treating the divorced in ways that are arbitrary or unscriptural.

It was never God's intention for people to rob one another. Robbery, like divorce, is the outworking of sin in the human heart. Nevertheless, robberies are committed, and both the Church and society recognize the obligation to deal with them in a just and realistic way. No sensible person takes this line: "Robbery is evil; therefore we must enforce the law against both parties. We will imprison both the person who committed the robbery and the person who was robbed." Obviously that would be a travesty of justice!

Yet in the matter of divorce, the Church has often taken a similar line, refusing to acknowledge a distinction between the innocent and the guilty party. "Divorce is evil," the Church has declared, "so we will impose the same penalty on both parties. We will forbid them both to remarry." In fact, the innocent party has been robbed of something more precious than material possessions; and the penalty imposed on such a person is more severe than a period of physical imprisonment.

Many religious people will be inclined to question the phrase *the innocent party.* Are not both parties to a divorce guilty? Should not both parties be treated the same?

It would be just as reasonable to suggest that both parties to a robbery are guilty and should be treated the same.

Again, some will ask: Does the Bible permit divorce on any grounds at all? The immediate answer to this question is a clear, unambiguous *yes.* In the time of Ezra, when some of the Jews had contravened the Law of Moses by marrying women from the surrounding Gentile nations, Ezra not only permitted them to divorce their wives; he actually demanded that they do so. (See Ezra 9–10.)

To get a scriptural perspective on situations in which one

party to a marriage may be released from the marriage bond, it is necessary to consider three successive phases of God's dealings with humanity: the period before the Law of Moses; the period under the Law of Moses; and the period inaugurated by Jesus through the Gospel.

The period before the law of Moses. In Israel before Moses, the penalty for adultery was death. This is illustrated by an incident in the life of Judah. At one point, Judah had sexual relations with a woman he believed was a prostitute, but who was actually his daughter-in-law Tamar. Tamar was at that time betrothed to Judah's youngest son, Shelah. The relationship of betrothal was considered as binding as marriage itself, and a breach of it was treated as adultery. Three months later it was discovered that Tamar was pregnant. Judah's immediate response was, "Bring her out and have her burned to death!" (Genesis 38:24). When he discovered that he himself was responsible for Tamar's pregnancy, he no longer demanded that she be put to death. Nevertheless, this incident makes it clear that the recognized penalty for adultery at that time was death.

The death penalty thus imposed on the guilty party in a marriage automatically released the innocent party to remarry.

The period under the Law of Moses. Under the Law of Moses the mandatory penalty for adultery, whether by man or by woman, was death (see Deuteronomy 22:22–24). Once again, the death penalty for the guilty party automatically released the innocent party to remarry.

People often quote Paul's statement in Romans 7:2, "By law a married woman is bound to her husband as long as he is alive. . . ." They fail to add that the same law that bound a wife to her husband for life, by imposing the death penalty on either party if guilty of adultery, automatically released the innocent party to remarry.

Furthermore, the New Testament emphasizes consistently that the Law of Moses must always be applied as a single, comprehensive system, all the requirements of which are equally valid. For example:

> For whoever keeps the whole law and yet stumbles at just one point is guilty of breaking all of it.
>
> (James 2:10)

> For it is written, "Cursed is everyone who does not continue to do everything written in the Book of the Law."
>
> (Galatians 3:10)

It is both illogical and unscriptural to uphold the requirement of the law that binds a woman to her husband for life, but to negate the requirement of the same law that automatically sets her free, through the death penalty, if her husband commits adultery.

The period inaugurated by Jesus through the Gospel. In the New Testament Jesus explicitly sanctioned divorce on the grounds of marital unfaithfulness:

> But I tell you that anyone who divorces his wife, except for marital unfaithfulness, causes her to commit adultery, and anyone who marries a woman so divorced commits adultery.
>
> (Matthew 5:32)

> I tell you that anyone who divorces his wife, except for marital unfaithfulness, and marries another woman commits adultery.
>
> (Matthew 19:9)

The Greek word translated "marital unfaithfulness" is *porneia*. Traditionally—e.g. in the King James Version—this word has been translated "fornication," thus limiting it to sexual sin by unmarried persons. Throughout the Greek New Testament, however, *porneia* is used to describe every form of illicit or unnatural sex. The following are some definitions of *porneia* given by recognized authorities.

It stands for, or includes adultery.
Expository Dictionary of New Testament Words
by W. E. Vine

Prostitution, unchastity . . . every kind of unlawful sexual intercourse . . . adultery appears as fornication. . . . The sexual unfaithfulness of a married woman. . . .
A Greek-English Lexicon of the New Testament
by Arndt & Gingrich

Illicit sexual intercourse in general. . . .
Thayer's Greek-English Lexicon

In the New Testament, *porneia* with its related verb *porneuo* is used in the following instances (among others), which cover more than sexual sin by unmarried persons.

In Acts 15:20, 29, Gentile Christians are commanded to abstain from *porneia*—clearly not merely from sexual sin by unmarried persons.

In 1 Corinthians 5:1, Paul describes a man living with his father's wife as *porneia*. Here it includes both incest and adultery.

In 1 Corinthians 5:9–11, Paul commands believers not to associate with professing Christians who are guilty of *porneia*. Obviously he does not limit this to unmarried persons. Paul uses *porneia* and *porneuo* in a similar way in 1 Corinthians 10:8 and 2 Corinthians 12:21.

In verse 7 of his epistle, Jude applies *porneia* to the sexual misconduct of Sodom and Gomorrah. The main sin of these cities was homosexuality, and there is no suggestion it was confined to unmarried persons.

It is clear, then, that *porneia* includes fornication, homosexuality, bestiality, incest, and adultery; and that Jesus sanctioned divorce (where appropriate) for any or all of these causes.

Thus, both the law and the gospel come to the same conclusion concerning *porneia:* it releases the innocent partner from his or her marriage obligations.

There is, however, a difference. Under the law, release is provided by the mandatory death penalty imposed on the guilty partner. Under the gospel, the innocent partner is free either to claim the release offered through divorce or to offer to the guilty partner the alternative of forgiveness and reconciliation, subject to satisfactory proof of repentance.

Is a person who has obtained a divorce on biblical grounds thereby free to remarry? Neither the language nor the culture of the Bible gives any hint that a person might be legally free only to divorce and not to remarry. On the contrary, freedom to remarry is stated explicitly in both the Old and the New Testaments.

Under the Law, Moses says that if a man divorces his wife legally and sends her away, she is free to become "the wife of another man" (Deuteronomy 24:1–2). Obviously Moses is not condoning adultery.

In Deuteronomy 24:3–4, Moses says that if the woman's second husband divorces her or dies, her first husband is not allowed to marry her again. By calling the man to whom she was previously married her "first" husband, Moses indicates clearly that the first marriage had been legally terminated.

In the New Testament Paul says: "Are you bound to a wife? Do not seek to be released. Are you released from a wife? Do not seek a wife. But if you should marry, you have not sinned . . ." (1 Corinthians 7:27–28, NASB).

This indicates that a person who is (scripturally) released from a marriage partner and later remarries *has not sinned.* No stigma of guilt or inferiority, therefore, should follow a person who obtains a divorce on legitimate, scriptural grounds and later exercises his or her right to remarry. Such a person is not a "second-class Christian."

On the human level, the issue of divorce is normally resolved in a court of law, either religious or secular. Beyond all such human decisions, however, lie divine principles of justice that never vary. One such principle runs throughout the entire Bible: *the innocent must never be treated as guilty, nor the guilty as innocent.*

In Deuteronomy 25:1 Moses succinctly sums up the double responsibility of judges—to acquit the innocent and to condemn the guilty. In Proverbs 17:15 Solomon indicates that any departure from this principle will meet with God's strong disfavor: "Acquitting the guilty and condemning the innocent—the Lord detests them both." Similarly, in a list of those who incur God's wrath, Isaiah says: "Woe to those . . . who acquit the guilty . . . but deny justice to the innocent" (Isaiah 5:22–23).

The application of this principle to the issue of divorce is obvious. To impose the same penalty on a marriage partner guilty of *porneia* and on one who is not denies the very nature of justice.

People sometimes argue that there are two sides to a marriage break-up and that it is not possible to know who the guilty partner really is. But this obscures the real question at issue. It is not whether there has been selfishness or insensitivity or quarreling on both sides. It is simply this: Has one partner committed *porneia* and the other not? In many cases today, one partner openly acknowledges his or her guilt.

God, at least, obviously envisaged the possibility that the guilt of one partner would be established, to the exclusion of the other; for under the Law of Moses He ordained the death of the proven adulterer or adulteress.

In one sense, marriage is a legal contract entered into by a vow. The extent of the contract is determined by the vow that is made. The marriage vow commonly used today goes something like this: "I plight thee my troth . . . to keep myself to thee alone [that is, in sexual relationship] . . . 'til death us do part."

In this vow there are two main elements: a use clause ("to keep myself to thee alone"); and a time clause ("'til death us do part"). These two clauses are tied to one another and cannot be enforced separately. Thus, if one partner breaks the use clause by *porneia*, the other partner is released automatically from the time clause.

Let me offer a simply worldly analogy. Smith leases a property to Brown on a five-year lease to run from 1986 to 1991. But he inserts one use clause: Brown may not use the property for a liquor store. If Brown abides by the use clause and refrains from using the property for a liquor store, then Smith must abide by the time clause; he cannot terminate the lease before 1991. But if Brown breaks the use clause by using the property for a liquor store, then Smith is automatically released from the time clause and can terminate the lease immediately.

Similarly, when one party to a marriage breaks the use clause by *porneia*, the other party is thereby released from the time clause—"till death us do part."

Under the ordinances of the New Testament, there is one further situation in which a Christian may be released from the marriage bond. It is described by Paul in 1 Corinthians 7:10–15:

> To the married I give this command (not I, but the Lord): A wife must not separate from her husband.

But if she does, she must remain unmarried or else be reconciled to her husband. And a husband must not divorce his wife.

To the rest I say this (I, not the Lord): if any brother has a wife who is not a believer and she is willing to live with him, he must not divorce her. And if a woman has a husband who is not a believer and he is willing to live with her, she must not divorce him. For the unbelieving husband has been sanctified through his wife, and the unbelieving wife has been sanctified through her believing husband. Otherwise your children would be unclean, but as it is, they are holy.

But if the unbeliever leaves, let him do so. A believing man or woman is not bound in such circumstances. . . .

In verses 10–11 Paul deals with the case of two believers married to one another. By his parenthesis—"not I, but the Lord"—he indicates that this case has already been covered by Jesus in His teaching recorded in the Gospels. The position is clear and unambiguous: Neither party is free to divorce the other, except for marital unfaithfulness. (Since Jesus stated this exception in the Gospels, there was no need for Paul to repeat it here.) If they do divorce, however, they are obligated to remain unmarried or to remarry each other.

In verses 12–15 Paul deals with the case of a believer married to an unbeliever. By his parenthesis—"I, not the Lord"—Paul indicates that this case was not covered by Jesus in the Gospels. First, Paul places on the believing party the obligation to seek to maintain peace in the marriage, and to win over the unbelieving party to faith in Christ. But when the unbelieving party rejects this approach and refuses to continue the marriage, but deserts the believer, then the believer is released from the marriage bond and thus freed to enter into a new marriage. There are, however, two conditions that must still be met. First, all requirements of the civil law must be fulfilled; and second, the new spouse must be a believer in Christ.

We have considered two cases dealt with explicitly in the New Testament: when one marriage partner is guilty of marital unfaithfulness; and when a believer is deserted by an unbeliever on the grounds of the believer's faith in Christ. In each of these cases, when all the relevant requirements have been met, the believer has the right to obtain a divorce and, as a consequence, also to remarry.

For readers who desire a more comprehensive study of divorce and remarriage in light of the Bible, I would recommend the book *Divorce and Remarriage* by Guy Duty.* The author, who up to his death in 1977 was an ordained minister of the American Assemblies of God, treats every aspect of his theme with a logical, legal exactness that leaves no questions unanswered.

There are other cases involving divorce, however, which are not explicitly covered in the New Testament. On the one hand, it is unrealistic to ignore such cases. On the other hand, it is unwise to be dogmatic where the Bible is not specific. Perhaps the best course for a sincere Christian minister is to say with Paul, "I have no command from the Lord, but I give a judgment as one who by the Lord's mercy is trustworthy" (1 Corinthians 7:25).

What about those with marital failure and divorce in their past, who then come to Christ for salvation? How does God view them?

Concerning the issue of forgiveness, the Bible is absolutely unambiguous (thank God!). In Matthew 12:31, for instance,

*Published by Bethany Fellowship, Minneapolis, 1967.

Jesus says: "And so I tell you, every sin and blasphemy will be forgiven men, but the blasphemy against the Spirit will not be forgiven." "Every sin" includes adultery and all other sexual deviations. The only exception is blasphemy against the Holy Spirit.

In Acts 13:39 Paul tells a Jewish audience: "Through him [Jesus] everyone who believes is justified from everything you could not be justified from by the law of Moses." Notice how comprehensive this is! *Everyone* is justified from *everything*. This includes adultery and all forms of sexual sin.

Again in 1 Corinthians 6:9–11 Paul writes to the believers in Corinth:

> Neither the sexually immoral nor idolaters nor adulterers nor male prostitutes nor homosexual offenders nor thieves nor the greedy nor drunkards nor slanderers nor swindlers will inherit the kingdom of God. And that is what some of you were. But you were washed, you were sanctified, you were justified in the name of the Lord Jesus Christ and by the Spirit of our God.

This ugly list of offenders includes adulterers and sexual perverts. Through faith in Christ they are not only forgiven; they are justified, acquitted, reckoned righteous with God's own righteousness. In God's sight it is as if they had never sinned. Surely this releases them to make a completely new start in every area of their lives, including that of marriage. No dark shadow of guilt or condemnation from their past can follow them into this new life.

Those who challenge the right of such repentant believers to a completely new start in life are in danger of ignoring the warning given to Peter in Acts 10:15: "Do not call anything impure that God has made clean."

The cases in which Christians are faced with the issue of

divorce are so numerous and complicated that it is impossible to examine them all in detail. The following are just three examples.

Case No. 1. Two unsaved divorcees marry, have children, and then get saved. Is it right to say to them: "You are living in adultery. You must break up your marriage, and either return to your former spouses or remain unmarried." What would happen to the children?

Is it not more in line with the spirit of the Gospel to say: "God has given you a new start. Do your best to redeem the misspent years and be careful not to go back to your old ways."

Case No. 2. Two unsaved people marry, then divorce, but not on grounds of marital unfaithfulness. After a while the man remarries, and thus commits adultery by scriptural standards. Later the woman gets saved. Is she free to remarry on the grounds that her previous husband has committed adultery?

Case No. 3. Two unsaved people marry, then divorce (as in Case No. 2). After divorce, they lose contact. The woman does not know whether the man has remarried or is living with a woman who is not his wife. Then the woman gets saved. Is she free to remarry? Or must she first prove that her previous husband has committed adultery? What if she is not able to make contact with him again?

Do we not all need to be very careful how we judge these (and similar) cases? Surely the principle that should guide us is stated in James 2:12–13: "Speak and act as those who are going to be judged by the law that gives freedom, because judgment without mercy will be shown to anyone who has not been merciful. Mercy triumphs over judgment!"

The above outline, though brief, covers some of the main

legal aspects of divorce, as it affects Christians. The effects of divorce, however, go far beyond the purely legal realm. Almost invariably they include deep, even agonizing emotional wounds.

In Isaiah 54:6 the Lord pictures a young woman who has been divorced: "A wife deserted and distressed in spirit—a wife who married young, only to be rejected." This kind of suffering is not confined to women who have been through divorce. Men, too, often suffer just as deeply as women.

In the passage from Isaiah, the Lord defines the precise nature of the wound. It is *rejection*. In God's marvelous grace, however, He offers a healing remedy for this wound. It is provided through the substitutionary sacrifice of Jesus on the cross, where Jesus endured vicariously all the evils that rebellion brought upon the human race. The final agony that caused His death was that of rejection.

The prophet Isaiah portrays Jesus as "despised and rejected by men, a man of sorrows" (Isaiah 53:3). The ultimate rejection, however, was not that by men, but by God, His Father. He endured this because He had become identified with the sin of humanity. In response, God's justice demanded that He turn away from His own Son and close His ears to His cry of agony.

This final rejection by the Father is described in Matthew 27:46: "About the ninth hour Jesus cried out in a loud voice, *'Eloi, Eloi, lama sabachthani?'*—which means, 'My God, my God, why have you forsaken me?'" For the first time in the history of the universe, the Father did not respond to His Son's cry. The death of Jesus that immediately followed was due to this agony of rejection, rather than to the physical effects of crucifixion, which would not have caused so rapid a death. Later Pilate, not understanding the effect of rejection, "was surprised to hear that [Jesus] was already dead" (Mark 15:44).

After Jesus' agonized cry to the Father, Matthew goes on to record: "And when Jesus had cried out again in a loud voice, he gave up his spirit" (verse 50).

The sufferings of Jesus were the price paid to obtain healing for humanity. "By his wounds we are healed" (Isaiah 53:5). Included in this provision is healing for the wound of rejection. Jesus endured rejection on our behalf that we in turn might be healed from it.

If through the break-up of a marriage you have experienced the wound of rejection, here are three simple steps by which you may receive healing.

First, acknowledge that you are hurting. Do not seek to cover up your wound. Be willing to expose it to the merciful eyes of your heavenly Father.

Second, put your faith for healing solely in the substitutionary sacrifice of Jesus. Apply the words of Isaiah personally to yourself: "By His wounds I am healed." Each time you begin to feel the pain, repeat the words, "By His wounds I am healed." Keep on saying it, until the healing becomes more real than the pain.

Third, lay down all bitterness and resentment against your former spouse. Forgiving the other party comes by decision, not emotion. You do not have to *feel* it; you have to *will* it. Invoke the help of the Holy Spirit to make and maintain the decision to forgive. Remember, the forgiveness you receive from God is commensurate with the forgiveness you offer to others (see Matthew 6:14–15).

I counseled a woman once whose husband had given her a miserable life for fifteen years, then abandoned her and the children. I urged her to forgive him.

"He's ruined fifteen years of my life," she exclaimed indignantly, "and you're asking me to forgive him?"

"Well, if you want him to ruin the rest of your life, too," I replied, "just keep on resenting him." I reminded her that the one who resents suffers more than the one who is resented.

Seen in this light, forgiving the one who has injured you is neither sentimentality nor lofty spirituality. It is simply enlightened self-interest.

When you have gone through these steps, turn your back on the hurts of the past. Make a fresh commitment of your whole life and future to the Lord. He has a plan for your life that cannot be frustrated by the malice of men or demons. Follow the example of Paul: "Forgetting what is behind and straining toward what is ahead, I press on toward the goal to win the prize for which God has called me heavenward in Christ Jesus" (Philippians 3:13–14).

Let me assure you that I have ministered personally to many divorcees who, by following these steps, have received healing of their wounds and renewed faith for a life of fruitfulness and fulfillment.

11

The Place of Celibacy

Marriage is the normal path in life for both men and women. God does not lead all His children, however, by the normal path. For the committed Christian, the ultimate purpose of life on this earth is not to get married; it is to do the will of God. Jesus established this pattern once and for all in John 4:34: "My food is to do the will of him who sent me and to finish his work." For Jesus Himself, the will of God did not include marriage during His life in the flesh. Rather, Jesus is looking forward to the day when He will celebrate His marriage with His Bride, the Church!

As Christians, we need to remind ourselves continually that perfection in its fullest sense is not to be attained in our present life here on earth. We cannot afford to become enamored of anything that is purely temporal. The apostle John warns us, "And the world is passing away, and also its lusts; but the one who does the will of God abides forever" (1 John 2:17, NASB). Lasting satisfaction and fulfillment in life have only one sure, unchanging foundation: to find and to do God's will.

Suppose God's will for your life does not include marriage. Suppose He is asking you to wait, like Jesus, for the marriage of the Lamb. What then?

Perhaps this is an issue you have never honestly faced. You have simply made marriage your goal and striven toward it— but without success up to now. You say, "I have prayed and prayed for a husband [or wife], but God has not answered." Are you forgetting that *no* is also an answer?

As you face this issue, it is essential to lay down your own plans and preconceptions and to open your heart to God. Often when God is ready to speak to us, we are not ready to hear what He has to say. God challenges us in Psalm 46:10: "Be still, and know. . . ." To this we need to respond with the words of Psalm 85:8: "I will listen to what God the Lord will say. . . ."

It will take time and sacrifice and self-discipline to come to that place of inner stillness in which you can hear God speak. It may mean less time in front of the television set, or on the phone with friends, or in social engagements. It may require laying aside newspaper or magazine and spending hours alone with the Bible. But whatever it takes, there is no substitute for hearing the voice of God. The cost may seem high, but the rewards far exceed the cost!

Of one thing you can be sure. If it is God's plan for you to be single, you will never find real peace or satisfaction as long as you are striving to be married. And if, after all, you eventually succeed in marrying, you will not solve your deep inner frustrations. On the contrary, you will probably increase them. Your unfortunate mate may also become a victim to them.

It may be that you have sincerely sought God concerning marriage, and He has not given you a definite answer one way or the other. He has not given you a mate, but He has not shown you that it is His will for you to remain single. If so, you need to follow the advice of David in Psalm 37:7–8: "Be still before the Lord and wait patiently for him. . . . Do not fret—it leads only to evil." Give yourself wholeheartedly to serving God in your present condition, and leave the future in His hands. Your attitude of quiet trust will keep you open to any direction the Lord may intend to give you farther down the road.

It is important for every unmarried Christian to face the issue of whether celibacy may be God's will for his or her life. A person who has settled this issue to his own satisfaction has an inner peace of mind that makes it easier to discern God's will in other matters, too. A person whose mind is taken up continually with thoughts of marriage, on the other hand, may miss God's leading in some other area and so take a wrong course in life.

What are the main reasons a Christian may need to remain single? They can be divided into two categories: natural and spiritual. Natural reasons, in most cases, apply equally to Christians and non-Christians. They originate in the way a person's life or circumstances have developed, without reference to any direct intervention of God. Spiritual reasons, on the other hand, relate to a Christian's special calling or field of service.

Natural reasons for celibacy may be subdivided into three categories: physical, psychological, and sociological. Physical reasons relate to the way a person's body has developed. Psychological reasons relate to the way a person's mind and emotions have developed. Sociological reasons relate to the kind of society in which a person lives. Since this is not a textbook in any of these fields—medical, psychological, or sociological—I am not attempting a detailed analysis of the kinds of problems that may arise.

Christians struggling with personal problems in any of these areas, however, would do well to pray about seeking advice from a qualified professional. If possible, such a professional should be a committed Christian, or at least sympathetic to the traditional Judeo-Christian ethic.

For the present, it is sufficient to glance at a few typical examples of natural reasons for celibacy. In the physical area, obvious cases might be those with severe congenital defects, such as Mongolism or cerebral palsy, or those who have suffered severe injuries, such as quadriplegics. Again, there are those whose sexual functions have not developed at all or have not developed normally. In many of these cases—but certainly not in all—the Lord may indicate it is best for such a person to remain single.

In the area of psychological problems, there are those who in popular speech are termed "simple." Some would probably be classified as retarded. Nearly every Christian congregation of any size has one or more of these. Often they are among the happiest and most lovable members. There are also those who would be categorized medically as schizophrenic or even psychotic. Out of the depths of their struggles, they manifest insight and devotion at times that are worthy of saints. Yet for these and others like them, celibacy often seems to be the Lord's plan.

Sociologically, there are various situations that may provide reasons for celibacy. One such case occurs in Ruth's family background. Her grandmother died at an early age, leaving six children. The youngest, a girl named Caroline, was about six at the time. Some years later Caroline's father remarried. Caroline remained at home to care for him and her stepmother. When Caroline was about 40, her father died. By this time her stepmother was crippled with arthritis. Caroline felt it was her duty to continue to care for her stepmother, until she too died nearly twenty years later. Caroline lived out the rest of her life single, having faithfully fulfilled her scriptural obligations to her parents.

Again, there are communities in various parts of the world in which the number of eligible Christian men is smaller than the number of committed Christian women in the same age bracket. In such a situation, many of the Christian women may wisely decide that it is better to remain single and give the Lord wholehearted devotion than to be unequally yoked with a man lacking in true spiritual commitment. Such dedicated single women are a source of tremendous spiritual strength in many local congregations.

Someone might be prompted to ask, "Can't God miraculously heal people with the kinds of physical and psychological problems mentioned above?" Certainly He can. Indeed, I have seen many people touched and transformed by the power of God, including those who were Mongoloid, paralyzed, schizophrenic, psychotic, and those with cerebral palsy.

At the same time, I must acknowledge that I have seen a greater number who were *not* healed. The same kinds of prayers were offered for those who were healed and for those who were not. Nor was there any reason to believe that those who were healed were in any way more sanctified or more dedicated than those who were not.

What is the explanation? For my part, I find a sufficient answer in Deuteronomy 29:29: "The secret things belong to the Lord our God, but the things revealed belong to us and to our children forever, that we may follow all the words of this law." The reason some of God's choicest children—yes, even His most effective servants—are not healed belongs to the realm of "the secret things," things God does not see fit to share with us at this time. I have learned to bow before His sovereignty and say, as Jesus Himself said: "Yes, Father, for this was your good pleasure" (Matthew 11:26).

I have also learned, by experience and observation, the truth of God's assurance to Paul: "My grace is sufficient for you" (2 Corinthians 12:9). When these words were spoken, Paul was in a situation of severe affliction from which God refused to deliver him. Instead, God supplied the grace that enabled him to triumph in the midst of affliction.

In such cases, the grace of God operates in one of two ways. It may deliver us marvelously *out* of the affliction. Or it may leave us *in* the affliction, but turn affliction into victory. Which way God's grace operates lies in each case within the sovereignty of His own will. But whichever way God chooses to act, His grace is always sufficient. Someone has expressed it this way: *The will of God will never place me where the grace of God cannot keep me.*

It would be a mistake to suppose that Christians who labor under afflictions that keep them from marrying never achieve the kind of peace or happiness enjoyed by other Christians. Strange though it may seem, the contrary is often true. Many Christians handicapped in some way achieve a greater measure of serenity and contentment than others considered "normal." The fact is, true peace and fulfillment come only to those who have learned to bow before the sovereign will of God, whether that will be wholeness or continuing affliction. Often this kind of surrender comes more quickly to "handicapped" Christians than to those who enjoy full mental and physical health.

The same is true of Christians who, because of circumstances in their family or community, choose not to marry. Often they prove to be happier and more fruitful in God's service than some of the married Christians around them.

When we move from natural to spiritual reasons for celibacy, the New Testament confronts us with two different possibilities. The first is produced by a sovereign, supernatural impartation of God; the second is achieved by the human will through a sacrificial act of self-renunciation.

The outstanding example of celibacy imparted supernaturally is that of the apostle Paul. Here is how he describes the reason for his celibate condition: "I wish that all men were as I am [that is, celibate]. But each man has his own gift from God; one has this gift, another has that" (1 Corinthians 7:7). For Paul, celibacy was not a sacrifice. It was a gift from God. He was *happy* in that condition. He would have been unhappy married.

The Greek word here translated "gift" is *charisma*. The plural form is *charismata*. It is the origin of the modern English word *charismatic*.

Charisma is one of the distinctive concepts of the New Testament and an essential element in its unique revelation. It is formed from the root word *charis*, with the addition of the final syllable *ma*. *Charis* means beauty, favor, grace; and refers particularly to the way God deals with those He accepts as His children on the basis of their faith in Jesus Christ. As such, grace can never be earned. It proceeds solely from the free and sovereign determination of God Himself.

The addition of the final syllable *ma* converts the general to the specific. *Charis* is "grace" generally, in all its various forms, while a *charisma* is a single, specific form of that grace, given to an individual Christian for the outworking of God's sovereign purpose in his or her life.

Over the past decades, the charismatic movement (as it has come to be known) has brought to God's people worldwide a new awareness of the place of charismata in the Christian life. One main effect has been to confront the Church afresh with the supernatural dimension of Christianity. Particular attention has been paid to the nine charismata, or spiritual gifts, listed in 1 Corinthians 12:8–10.

Many charismatic believers are under the impression that these are all the charismata there are available. This is far from being true. I have counted 22 specific manifestations of God's grace mentioned in the New Testament, all called charismata.

One of these, mentioned by Paul in 1 Corinthians 7:7, is celibacy. When teaching on the charismatic gifts, I have sometimes warned Christians that if they merely ask God for some charisma, without being specific, they may find He blesses them with the charisma of celibacy! Most of them are not even aware that this, too, is a charisma.

This simple analysis of the word *charisma* reveals two important facts about the nature of Paul's celibacy. First of all, it was a sovereign gift from God. It was not something Paul had earned, or could earn. Nor was it a decision that he himself arrived at. God in His unsearchable wisdom bestowed the gift on Paul. Paul, in turn, received it and used it for the purpose for which God gave it.

Second, Paul's celibacy was on a plane higher than the natural. It was not something he had achieved by his own efforts. It was not the outcome, for example, of a rigorous course of asceticism. Certainly it required self-discipline to keep the gift inviolate and use it for its divinely ordained purpose. But no amount of self-discipline alone could have produced the gift in the first place. It came only by a supernatural impartation from God.

It is important to see, too, that Paul's celibacy did not cut him off from the Body of Christ, or even from the pressures and challenges of life in this world. He was continually in the midst of people—both the people of God and the people of the world. Paul himself wrote concerning spiritual gifts: "Now to each one the manifestation of the Spirit is given for the common good" (1 Corinthians 12:7). This was true of his own gift of celibacy. It was not merely a narrow path to his own spiritual perfection. Its purpose was to equip him in the most effective way for the upbuilding of the whole Body of Christ.

In 1 Corinthians 9:5-6, Paul contrasts the special ministry he and Barnabas had with that of the other apostles: "Don't we have the right to take a believing wife along with us, as do the other apostles and the Lord's brothers and Cephas? Or is it only I and Barnabas who must work for a living?" We can take this to indicate that Barnabas, like Paul, was unmarried. Clearly, however, these two were the exceptions among the apostles. The rest had wives who normally traveled with them on their ministry journeys.

Obviously there was a direct relationship between Paul's celibacy and the special pressures and demands of his God-appointed ministry. It was an essential tool for what he had to do. If Paul had been married, one of two results would inevitably have followed: either his marriage would have been a disaster, or he would not have accomplished his life task.

It is easy for me to believe that John Wesley was endowed by God with a similar gift, but failed to perceive it. His marriage may have been the only major mistake of his life. It hindered rather than helped his ministry and seems to have provided him with no personal happiness or fulfillment. It is important, therefore, for God's servants to be able to discern the special type of calling that needs to be equipped with a gift of celibacy.

In Matthew 19:12, Jesus refers to another type of celibacy that also has a place in the Christian life: "For some are eunuchs because they were born that way; others were made that way by men; and others have renounced marriage [literally, *have made themselves eunuchs*] because of the kingdom of heaven."

Jesus describes as eunuchs those incapable of the normal sexual relationship. He specifies three different ways this may come about. Some are born like this; some are made like this by a human act (that is, castration); and some achieve this condition by a decision of their own will.

These last do it "because of the kingdom of heaven"—that is, to be able to devote themselves without reservation to service in God's Kingdom. Although the word *eunuch* is normally restricted to males, it seems appropriate to include in this category both men and women who, for the sake of God and His Kingdom, have renounced marriage and given themselves to special forms of Christian service in a condition of celibacy. Obviously, the history of the Church through the centuries provides countless examples of "eunuchs" of this kind.

People in this third category, however, have not been endowed with a supernatural charisma of celibacy. This is indicated by the language Jesus uses: they have *made themselves* eunuchs. Their condition proceeds from their own decision, not from a sovereign act of God. Such people, unlike Paul, could have been happy married. For them, celibacy represents a sacrificial self-renunciation, achieved and maintained by the power of their own will.

On the spiritual plane, then, celibacy may come in one of two ways: as a charisma sovereignly imparted by God; or as a decision of the human will. In either case, the results it produces are connected with the inner, intricate mechanism of human personality.

The different forms of motivation and expression that make up a person may be compared to a number of rivers all fed from one lake. If one of the rivers is dammed, a correspondingly greater volume of water will be released through the others. One main river of human personality is the normal expression of sex in marriage. In the life of a Christian, however, if this river of sex is dammed, a correspondingly greater volume of spiritual, intellectual, and emotional energy may be released to other forms of expression—such as intercession, scholarship, artistic creativity, or service to the poor.

This is aptly summarized by Selwyn Hughes in an analysis of the place of sex in Christian living:

Surrender of the sex drive to God breaks its tyranny and its power. Alexis Carrel says that the people who do the greatest work in the world are strongly-sexed people who subordinate sex to the ends for which they live. In marriage the sex drive must be channelled into procreation and the giving of pleasure to one's partner. Outside of marriage, the sex drive must be sublimated and channelled into creativity in the kingdom of God. Remember—the strongly-sexed can strongly serve.*

Is there some special class of Christians who always need to remain celibate? Is it, for instance, a requisite for all called to the pastoral ministry? The New Testament gives no indication of this. It has already been pointed out that, among the apostles, the only two who had this special gift were Paul and Barnabas. (It could even be questioned whether Barnabas should be included.)

In the list of requirements for an overseer (traditionally translated *bishop*), Paul states: "Now the overseer must be . . . the husband of but one wife. . . . He must manage his own family well and see that his children obey him with proper respect" (1 Timothy 3:2, 4). Thus, far from requiring celibacy, Paul assumes that an overseer (or bishop) should be a married man with a family.

My own experience and observation over the years have convinced me that this is a wise and practical requirement. In dealing with single women and with married couples, a pastor often needs the special insight a wife can give him from her different perspective. He needs the protection of a wife, too, in situations in which he might otherwise be exposed to sexual temptation. It is unfair for a minister to have to spend

*Quoted from "Every Day With Jesus" for Friday, July 27, 1984.

much time alone with women, whether counseling or praying with them. Many undesirable and entangling relationships have developed out of such situations.

Undoubtedly these are some of the reasons why Judaism requires that a rabbi be a married man. In this respect, the Jewish position is closer to the Bible than the traditional Christian teaching that required celibacy in all clergy.

Celibacy certainly has a special place in God's provision for His ministering servants. It may come either as a sovereign charismatic impartation from God, or by a decision made prayerfully by an individual Christian. It is not, however, a standard requirement for all God's ministers in some particular category.

Concerning either marriage or celibacy, therefore, each person called to any form of ministry needs to discover the will of God for his or her own life.

Ruth's Story

12

"Meet Me in the King David"

My hand trembled. My heart was jumping as I stood beside my post office box in Jerusalem. I tore open the telegram. "Meet me in the King David Hotel at nine o'clock on 20 September. Prince."

I let out my breath and read the telegram again. Derek Prince was really coming to Jerusalem for Yom Kippur (the Day of Atonement—the most holy day of the Jewish year), and he wanted to see me!

I hurried back to my room at a nearby hospice and fell on my knees by the narrow bed, my Bible open before me beside the telegram. "Lord, does this mean what I think it means?" I prayed. "Quiet the pounding of my heart. Help me to hear Your voice, to wait for Your direction."

As I waited before Him, peace began to come—a quiet assurance that God was guiding me into the plan for which He had been preparing me.

Other questions still nagged: How could Derek Prince, whom I considered a great man of God, approach me, a divorced woman? What if I was imagining things—that it

was not the Lord at all who had been speaking to me these
last months? What if I was deceived? What if I let my hopes
rise, released my emotions, and then was wounded again? Did
I dare to trust him? Or any man?

I remembered so vividly that night in 1965. I had tossed
and turned in my bed, sobbing. My hopes and dreams of
"living happily ever after" had perished before my eyes. My
heart was torn, my emotions confused. I wanted to hope that
night that I could build a new life, find satisfaction and
fulfillment. Yet fear rose up in me—fear that I would never be
loved or be able to love again, that the remainder of my life
would be spent in solitude and loneliness. Or, even worse, in
another broken marriage.

I was what Scripture calls "a wife deserted and distressed in
spirit—a wife who married young, only to be rejected"
(Isaiah 54:6). At age 21 I had married a Jewish man. I had
converted to his religion, turning away from my own heritage
and culture. I had given myself without reservation to a
relationship I expected to last a lifetime. I had believed our
love could withstand every trial. Then, after thirteen years, it
was over. I didn't please him anymore. He didn't want me any
longer. He had found another woman. Our marriage had
ended.

Finally my sobs subsided and I slept. And with dawn came
the realization that a decision had somehow been made while
I slept. I would walk alone. Never again would I let myself
become vulnerable to the emotions and actions of another
person. I would keep my relationships superficial. I would not
let anyone close enough to hurt me like this again.

That was in 1965. Now it was 1977, and I had to decide
whether I dared to risk another intimate relationship. Because
I was a woman, I had to wait for the man to move before I
could even know if this was a possibility. This telegram
seemed to be a sure sign that Derek Prince was making that
move.

I could avoid the risk. I didn't have to respond. The only address he had was my postbox. If I didn't meet him at the King David, that would be the end of it. But would that please God? Did I dare to disobey the inner voice that said, *This is why I brought you to live in Jerusalem. This is what I have been preparing you for, all your life.*

I waited quietly until full peace came. I did know I could trust my God, who had revealed Himself to me through Jesus, the Messiah. So I said, "Lord, may Your will in this matter be done. I don't know what lies ahead, but You do, and I trust You."

I had not always approached decisions this way. Born into a large family during the Depression, endowed with a good mind and a strong body, I had learned early to think for myself, to take the initiative, to rely on my own abilities. Many times I failed, falling short of my own expectations. My response was always the same: Set your will, study more, work harder, do better next time. Sometimes I was almost overwhelmed by emotional battles I could not overcome by willpower or self-discipline. But it never occurred to me to call on Jesus for help.

The Lutheran church in Michigan, where I grew up, somehow failed to impart to me the concept of a *personal* relationship with God. There were many activities—Sunday school, church suppers, confirmation classes, youth groups. But I never understood the Resurrection, and often became confused since Jesus and Martin Luther seemed to possess approximately equal status. Much later in life I learned that my younger brother had met Jesus in that church as a boy, so it was probably I who failed to understand what was being taught. At any rate, I left as soon as I was able to, concluding that religion had nothing to offer me.

A few years later, while serving as a sergeant in the U.S. Marine Corps, I met and married my Jewish husband.

Amazingly, as I studied to convert to his religion, I discovered the God I had never known in the Lutheran Church—not in a personal way, but in the assurance that there *was* a God who cared for the universe, and who for His own reasons had set His hand on the Jewish people. This was in the early 1950s, just after the Holocaust, and I struggled to understand the unique calling of the Jewish people—seemingly loved by God, yet suffering as no other people on earth.

The rabbi said to me, "Are you very sure you want to go through with this conversion? It is not easy to be a Jew. Nobody understands you. You may end up in a gas chamber. You are already married to your husband. Nobody will hold it against you if you do not complete the conversion. Be *very* sure!"

My answer was clear: I had found more in Judaism than I had believed could be found in religion. So I took the name *Ruth, "daughter of Abraham,"* and became an observant Conservative Jewess. I learned by rote the Hebrew prayers for the Sabbath and Jewish holidays. I learned how to cook the foods for special meals, how to prepare the home for different festivals. There was security and a measure of peace in the ritual, and even more in the relationships in the closely knit Jewish community.

Four Jewish children came to us, by adoption since I was not able to bear children. One of them, a daughter, lies buried in a Jewish cemetery in Portland, Oregon. I had found her one morning, dead in her bed, a "crib death." Somehow my newfound faith carried me through the shock and grief.

We moved many times during thirteen years of marriage, always to further my husband's career. Our anchor was either the local synagogue or other Jewish families in towns too small for a synagogue. We seemed to represent a typical Jewish family, prosperous, active in politics and our local community, busy with our social life. I was zealous for the

Jewish education of the children. I often drove them many miles for their lessons and attempted to shield them from the pressures of a predominantly Christian society.

Then one day my husband returned from a business trip. He unpacked and left the papers from his pocket on the dresser. A motel receipt caught my eye: Mr. *and Mrs.* Baker. Shocked, I picked it up. But there was no mistake. Things began to fall into place: "business" trips that extended over weekends, little interest in the children, criticism of me, measuring me against some unknown standard. My husband had found another woman.

When I recovered from the shock, I went to a trusted friend (a few years older than I) for advice. Her counsel was faultless: Say nothing, get your hair done, buy some new lingerie, fix his favorite meals, win him back.

For several months I pretended I knew nothing, welcomed him at every homecoming with open arms, wooed him. He liked it, but the other relationship continued. By this time I had learned who she was. The prospect of a transfer to another city gave me hope until he mentioned casually that she was moving, too. Then he told me how much the children had come to love her. This was too much—that when he took the children on outings without me, he had been including her! I went to see a lawyer.

The three years that followed were agony. Our whole life fell apart. Acquiescing to his request not to divorce him on grounds of adultery for the sake of his career, I agreed to a legal separation to be followed by a routine divorce. We divided the property, and the children and I moved into an older, smaller home, though still in a good neighborhood. I continued studies to complete my college degree.

Our arrangements were amicable, and I had no idea that when he was transferred out-of-state (and out of the jurisdiction of the court), he would stop alimony and child support payments.

It seemed then that I had lost everything except my children. I had no husband, no money, no hope—and now I must take up a legal battle. So I set my will, applied for a college loan, swallowed my pride, and found a part-time job selling cosmetics door-to-door. My goal was the salary I could earn when I finished my degree.

My children suffered even more. Deprived of a father, they now had a mother who was always too tired or too busy. Many nights I looked at them in their beds and cried inwardly, "Why, God? Why?" They had been such beautiful babies. We had brought them home with so much hope. But I could not be both mother and father to them. I could not even be the good mother I wanted to be. So I went on from day to day, doing the best I could under the circumstances.

Then real disaster struck: I became ill. The divorce had just become final, child support payments were coming again, I was almost ready to graduate. I thought I could relax a little—and now this! Surgery was followed by a sprained ankle, then a terrible bout with the flu. My situation looked impossible.

So one afternoon I lay in bed and cried out to the God of Abraham, Isaac, and Jacob: "Where are You, God? Don't You care about me? I can't care for myself or my children. I can't go on. Help me!"

Suddenly the whole atmosphere in my room became electric. There was a Presence there, powerful, comforting, peaceful. Jesus healed me. I knew it was Jesus. As a Jewess, I didn't even *believe* in Jesus—but He healed me anyway! Then the Presence was gone. My room was normal again. Dazed, I lay there a few minutes, then arose to test my strength. When the children came home from school, I was in the kitchen baking cookies.

It was wonderful to be well again. I plunged into all my activities, and was soon busy my usual eighteen hours a day. I didn't want to stop long enough to think; the implications of the revelation of Jesus were more than I could face.

I saw myself as a modern-day Ruth, totally committed to the God of Israel and the people of Israel. Now I believed in Jesus. What could I do? Mine was the most extraordinary experience I had ever heard of. I thought I was the first Jewish person who had ever believed in Jesus as the Messiah. I had no idea that individual Jews all over the world were also having personal encounters with the risen Messiah.

All I knew was that Jesus had healed me, and that I believed in Him. But I couldn't talk about it. My Jewish friends would be offended if I mentioned the name of Jesus in such a connection. I refused to read the New Testament given me by a new friend, a Christian with whom I had shared my story. I was afraid to seek any further understanding because of my loyalty to Judaism and the Jewish people.

For two years I ran from God. I showed no gratitude to the One who had healed me. I hardened my heart and refused to think about spiritual things. I gave all my energy to raising my children, developing my career, pursuing community activities, and keeping up my social life. I kept my mind occupied night and day.

All went well until 1970. Then my health failed again. Gall bladder surgery was scheduled. The pain was excruciating. And I was afraid. I remembered my lengthy illness two years before, and the relief when Jesus healed me so that I could resume a productive life. I didn't see how I could expect a second miracle now. I had not given Jesus as much respect as I gave my doctor, nor had I made any effort to learn what He taught about how to live in health. How little I knew about the mercy and compassion of God!

The day before the operation, I read the book *Face Up with a Miracle* by Don Basham, given me by my Christian friend. And for the first time, I saw clearly my need of a Savior—not just to heal me so I could continue on the course I had charted, but to cleanse my sin and give me a new God-directed life. I saw in particular my need for the power of the Holy Spirit to live that life—because I knew by now that I could not overcome every obstacle by sheer willpower and hard work. My pain-wracked body told me I had to make a radical change in my way of life.

There in the hospital room, I bowed my head and closed my eyes. Jesus had said, "Him that cometh to me I will in no wise cast out" (John 6:37, KJV). Simply, humbly, I came to Him. "Forgive me for sinning against You," I said, "for going my own way. Come into my heart."

And He did. It was uncomplicated, unemotional, as if I had made a verbal agreement with Jesus and we had shaken hands to seal the matter.

Then I said to Jesus, "If the baptism in the Holy Spirit is from You, and You want me to have it, I want it."

My new-found Master took me at my word, and strange syllables began to come to my tongue. In a whisper, lest I should be heard, I began to speak a new language I had never learned, a language given me from heaven. It was like a bubbling stream. Far into the night I lay whispering the syllables that welled up and out of me. They seemed to flow over me as a brook flows over stones: every note, every syllable washed me cleaner.

The next day I underwent surgery. Three weeks later I returned to work. Healing was swift; my recovery amazed me. Meanwhile, I had begun to read the Bible with hunger such as I had never known for anything. After an unemotional beginning, I had fallen in love with Jesus. Nothing satisfied me except His Word, and prayer in my new language.

Now I had another problem. I wrestled with the tension between the demands of my work in a civic organization and this new love that increased daily.

One night four months later, Jesus took me one step farther. He made it plain that I had to surrender myself entirely to Him. This was a struggle. My will was well-developed and strong. Finally I acknowledged that my life was not a tremendous success. True, I had graduated *cum laude* from college while raising three children and working part-time. True, my career prospects were excellent. But my health had failed twice in two years. I was finding it increasingly difficult to cope with my teenage son. I needed the inner peace I had found in Jesus. It seemed to me there was no alternative.

Even though my mind kept saying, "What if? What if?" with my will I surrendered. In my bedroom on February 21, 1971, I said to the Lord: "I'm forty years old, I'm not strong, I'm tired, I have a broken marriage, I have children who have problems—I don't know what You can do with me. But for whatever use I am to You, I give myself to You." And He accepted me.

Two nights later, as I began to pray, God answered me. I nearly fell out of bed. No one had ever told me that God speaks to people today. Again, I thought I was the first person to whom it had ever happened. It was awesome. I wondered why I had been chosen for such an experience. For twenty minutes I asked questions about my life and He answered me. He in turn required certain changes in my life. He told me He expected obedience, and indicated He would direct me so long as I was faithful to obey whatever I understood.

The conversation went on until I asked a question about someone else. He did not admonish me. He simply did not answer. I learned that lesson quickly: Don't be a busybody!

The new life I took up the next day astonished me. Doubts and fears had vanished. I was able to make every change God had asked in absolute assurance that He would stand behind me. During my years alone I had become a very independent person. Now, overnight, I had learned a new dependence on the Holy Spirit. I knew I could not obey the Lord unless I heard His voice; a holy awe and fear kept me seeking Him lest I should fail for lack of attentiveness. Only later did I realize that I had received a gift of the Holy Spirit—the gift of faith. With that gift I was able to step out of the position I held and wait for God to place me where He wanted me.

Over the next months, every day was an adventure as I learned to hear God's voice and act in obedience. He taught me flexibility, to change directions in response to the Holy Spirit. He gave me His love, flowing over me and through me to others.

My new work, as a Manpower Administrator for the State of Maryland, required extensive traveling, and my car became a mobile sanctuary. To this day, when I get into a car, my first desire is to sing. The Lord gave me a voice to praise Him and filled my heart with a song. I sang in the Spirit and I sang with my understanding. I prayed in the Spirit and I prayed with my understanding.

My relationship with Jesus was more real than my earthly relationships. I sought Him daily, and He never kept me waiting. The joy of communion with Him so far excelled any earthly emotion that I cannot even describe it. I suppose you could say it was a time of courtship with my heavenly Bridegroom, a foretaste of the real honeymoon that will begin with the marriage supper of the Lamb.

As the relationship deepened, and as I learned to know His voice more clearly, responding immediately to His direction, Jesus led me into intercessory prayer. I began to speak to Him very naturally about people and situations that concerned me, and He would show me how to pray. At first I was amazed by clear answers to prayer; then I realized He delights to answer the prayers of those who meet His conditions.

As I delighted myself in the Lord, as the psalmist

admonished in Psalm 37:4, He filled me more and more with Himself. He also met my needs through people: He gave me mature Christian couples as friends; other single women with whom I could pray; young men as friends to provide a masculine viewpoint without emotional involvement or compromise; a pastor with a real shepherd's heart; anointed teachers (one of whom was Derek Prince) through books, cassettes, and conferences. My life was full.

Then in 1974, during my first visit to Jerusalem, God called me to Israel. The burden for Israel had come during my first reading of the Bible, when I had reached Isaiah and Jeremiah. At that point I had understood the birth of the State of Israel, and had begun to pray every day for God to establish Jerusalem and make her the praise of the earth (Isaiah 62:6–7). The Yom Kippur War in 1973 had torn at my heart. I wanted to do more than pray. I wanted to help.

Still, I was unprepared when God spoke clearly to me to leave everything behind, and move to Israel. Remembering the night in 1971 when I had surrendered to Him, I knew He would direct me only so long as I was obedient to what I understood. I thought I knew His voice. Still, it was a risk. It was so far from anything I had ever thought of doing. Again my mind asked, *What if . . . ? What if . . . ?*

But God said no more. It was a decision I had to make. Finally I responded, "Yes, Lord. If that is what You want, it is what I want." I went back home, sought the counsel of my pastor for confirmation, then set out to obey.

It was the greatest test of my faith up to that time. The arrangements did not all go smoothly. My ex-husband, who had remarried and had a new family, knew of my faith in Messiah. He put every obstacle he could in my way when I asked his consent to take our youngest daughter, Erika, with me to Israel. When departure time was delayed, the enemy was there to whisper, *Hath the Lord really said . . . ?* I had to distinguish between natural problems, Satanic opposition, and God's testing of my resolve.

I learned to know Jesus in new dimensions. I had given away my possessions, resigned from my job, moved out of my home. As the delay continued for six months, I sought the Scriptures with renewed earnestness. The answer came in many verses: *Trust Me.*

When the test had accomplished His purposes, God took us to Jerusalem. It was a glorious homecoming. Not only had He brought Erika and me to the land of my adopted fathers, but He had vindicated His faithfulness. I was 44 years old, strong, healthy, filled with joy. Jesus had done so much for me in four years. Now He had brought me to His city—the City of the Great King! How could I want anything else? I was truly delighted in Him.

Two-and-a-half years later I lay in bed in my home in Jerusalem, where the Israeli doctors had sent me to rest, crippled by a ruptured disc in my back that would not heal. My spine, curved from childhood, would no longer support my body. Months went by without relief from the constant pain. I left my bed for one or two hours each day, but there was no evidence of improvement.

In my idle hours one afternoon I leafed through the notebook I kept of my conversations with the Lord. There it was: On November 4, 1976, wondering how I could better please and serve the Lord, I had recommitted myself to Him. On a plain sheet of paper I had drawn up a contract, acknowledging what He had done for me through the blood of Jesus and how far He had brought me from the day in 1971 when I yielded fully to Him. For my part, I stated that I had given myself to Him without reservation; and I had left the rest of the page blank for Him to fill in the conditions. I had signed it at the bottom.

So now I lay in bed. This was a "condition" I had not anticipated. I thought that after He saved me, He would keep me well for His service. Now I was helpless, in continual pain. On the positive side, my fellowship with Him was glorious. From early in the morning until late at night I stayed in the presence of Jesus. Flat on my back, I could hold the Bible just long enough to read brief snatches. I wore out the cassettes that played the Scriptures for me in those months. The healing I longed for did not come, but the inner conversation with Him and the sweetness of His presence were unbroken.

Then one day Derek Prince knocked on my door. He was in Jerusalem, had heard about me, and came to offer prayer for the healing of my back. I was overwhelmed. Though I had been secure for years in Jesus' love, it was hard to believe He would send a man of such stature to my door to pray for me.

Fortunately, I was not overawed by Derek. For twenty years I had been active in U.S. politics, and included senators, congressmen, and governors in my circle of acquaintances. I had tremendous respect for people in positions of authority, as do most of my generation, but at the same time could relax and behave naturally with them.

I invited him in, along with the young man with him. We talked together, first about my injury, and then about Jerusalem. I looked on Derek with real concern and compassion. He looked much older than his 62 years. His arm was in a cast, broken in a fall. His wife had died two years before, and I could still see the grief and loneliness on his face. It was hard to believe this was the strong, vital man I had heard preach so powerfully a few years before.

He offered to pray for me. I knew he had a special ministry of "lengthening legs" because it had happened to me in a large meeting in 1971. At that time, Derek did not yet fully understand the gift of faith God had given him, but now he explained that I must "keep the plug in" to God's miracle-working power by continuing to thank God that He had touched me.

As Derek held my feet in his hands he said, "They're perfectly level! Did anybody ever pray for you this way?"

"Yes," I replied. "You did, in 1971."

He chuckled. "I did a good job!" He stood beside me and put his hand on my shoulder.

Then, to my amazement, he began to prophesy. The message was one of encouragement from God, telling me I was a tree of His planting and that nothing would uproot me. What amazed me was that God had given me almost the exact words privately less than a week before, and I had written them in my notebook.

At the door Derek turned and said, "Keep the plug in! Keep thanking God." Then he added, "Pray for me. I'm going to Munich in West Germany next week for meetings. It's not an easy place to preach." Then he was gone.

I went back to bed and lay there thanking God. I was still overwhelmed that God had sent him. I appreciated Derek's kindness and sensitivity to the Holy Spirit. Most of all, I appreciated this sign from the Lord that He was hearing my prayers and that He wanted to heal me.

Nothing dramatic happened at once. When the pain became acute I would cry out, "Thank You, Jesus, that Your miracle-working power is at work in my body." My strength remained minimal. I could bathe and dress myself, but little more. I performed the exercises prescribed by the physical therapist. I swam from time to time at the public pool, my weak back supported by the water.

My daughter, then 17, and preparing to return to the U.S.A. for college, was reluctant to leave me in my invalid condition. Finally I agreed to accompany her to the States, and arranged my ticket so that I would return to Jerusalem the day before Rosh Hashana, the Jewish New Year. The airline promised a wheelchair at either end, and graciously allotted four seats to me so that I could lie down the whole way.

A week before departure I received a surprise—a handwritten letter from Derek Prince in which he mentioned a group in Kansas City who were very interested in Israel. He invited me to visit them if I were ever in the States. *What a kind man,* I thought. *He saw my need for rest and recuperation.* I had no thought that he had anything else in his mind. It never occurred to me that he was an eligible man. If it had, I probably would have responded differently.

I had no desire to marry anyone. My relationship with Jesus was totally satisfying. I lived to please Him. During those months of inactivity, I had discovered that intercession was the most effective service I could give Him. Each day I made myself available to Him to pray—for anyone or any situation He put on my heart. Many prayers I prayed, especially for Israel, were answered before my eyes. (Others are still being answered.)

I wrote a note to Derek Prince to thank him, gave him a phone number in Maryland where he could reach me, and arranged to arrive in Kansas City on August 20 for twelve days. Scarcely had I arrived in Maryland when he telephoned! I was stunned. He inquired after my health and told me he would see me in Kansas City. A few days later he called again. He sounded so friendly, so warm. I knew him as a pulpit personality with tremendous authority. His humanity surprised me.

Meanwhile, I was beginning to grow stronger. Some friends took me to a campground and installed me in their camper so I could be alone for a few days, lie in the sun, swim, and mainly seek God concerning the future. I would be returning to Israel without my daughter. My financial resources were limited. I needed to be clear about God's will.

I left that place of quiet assured that my responsibility to God was to continue as an intercessor, and that He had already prepared the means to provide for me. I didn't know how, but I was at peace.

As my friends drove me back to their home, they told me Derek Prince had called again. Whatever could he want? The travel arrangements were perfectly clear. Perhaps they were withdrawing the invitation?

But when I returned the call, he simply asked after my health. I told him I had been resting and swimming.

"Are you a good swimmer?" he asked.

I answered in the affirmative, but thought, *What kind of question is that for a Bible teacher to ask a lady?*

Then he said, "I phoned to let you know that my plane will arrive in Kansas City five minutes after yours. I'll be there only two days. I am due to leave for South Africa on August 23."

When I went downstairs after our phone call, my friend looked at me quizzically. "Are you free to say what he had on his mind?"

"It was strange," I replied. "He seemed just to want to get acquainted. He even asked if I was a good swimmer!"

She looked at me. "Do you think there is something more to this?"

I dropped my eyes. "I'm afraid to think about it."

Several times over the next few days, I brought this before the Lord. I could not understand why Derek Prince was approaching me. He had mentioned he was seeking God's will as to whether it was time for him to return to Jerusalem. I wondered if God wanted me to use my secretarial skills to work for him there. But I was in no condition to work. I had nothing to offer anyone on earth. All I had was the ability to pray, and I had given myself to the Lord for that purpose.

I had read Derek's book *Shaping History through Prayer and Fasting** and had heard some of his messages on intercessory prayer. Perhaps God was indicating we might pray together. But I didn't see how that could be. So much was unclear. Finally I left it with the Lord and went to Kansas City with an open mind.

Derek's plane was late, so his friend settled Erika and me in the backseat of the car with his wife, and went back to get Derek and his luggage. As Derek strode toward us, he again appeared the strong vibrant person I had seen at Bible conferences several years before, looking at least ten years younger than he had in Jerusalem only two months earlier.

He got into the front seat, and as he turned to greet us, he gave me a long, searching look. Outwardly I was calm, inwardly I was trembling. My inner questions to the Lord brought only one answer: *Trust Me.*

Erika and I were guests in his friends' spacious home, and Derek asked them to put a mattress on the floor for me to sleep on for the sake of my back. His practicality and understanding surprised me. Later I learned something of how he had cared for Lydia, who was much older than he, in her last years. He was very different than I had imagined.

I saw him very little in those two days. We ate with the family and had only one private conversation, in which I asked his advice about a situation in Jerusalem. He was very businesslike, though he did give me his two latest books and inscribed them for me—one *With my prayers* and the other *With my love,* (mentally I inserted *Christian* to make it *Christian love*).

His final evening I sat on Derek's right at dinner. When I looked at him, I realized I felt absolutely nothing. I had

---

*Published by Derek Prince Ministries, Fort Lauderdale, Florida, 1973.

tremendous respect for him as a man of God and anointed Bible teacher, but I did not expect to see him again personally. I felt honored by the attention he had shown me, but assumed this was the end of it.

The next morning as he was leaving for the airport, he turned to me and asked, "Have you decided definitely to return to Jerusalem?" I told him I would be there for Rosh Hashana. He said he was planning to come for Yom Kippur, and perhaps he would see me. And that was that.

Or was it?

In the next ten days I swam, walked, and did my exercises, carrying on a continual inner conversation with the Lord. Behind the house was a small brook with a wooden bridge. I would go out at night and pace back and forth on the bridge in the moonlight, spreading the thoughts of my heart out before the Lord. I knew I must obey Proverbs 4:23: "Keep thy heart with all diligence; for out of it are the issues of life" (KJV).

I could not afford to release my emotions, either to hope or to fear. It seemed to me now that God was saying He wanted me to be Derek's wife, but Derek had given me no indication of that kind of interest—except for the inscription in the book. Whether or not I was hearing correctly, I had to decide what I would do if this *was* the case. On the one hand, it would be a tremendous honor to be Derek's wife—and a great responsibility. If this was God's plan, then He must intend to heal me, to make me strong physically as well as spiritually.

Again, I would count the cost. My last child was leaving the nest. I was ready to enjoy a degree of personal liberty I had not known for twenty-five years, responsible to and for no other person. More important, I had no desire to marry again. It was twelve years since my husband had left me, seven years since I had met Jesus. My life with the Lord was full and satisfying. Yet . . . if God wanted me to marry, dare I refuse?

Then a deluge of questions: Could I risk letting someone else into my heart and life? Even more frightening: Could I be a good wife? What if I was unable to adjust to his ways and habits? What if, after all these years alone, I could not put his needs before mine? What if I could not be flexible? I knew he traveled widely. What if I could not keep up the pace? My back was stronger, but I was by no means well. What about my privacy—those hours I cherished alone with the Lord? And what would it do to Derek Prince's reputation to marry a divorcee?

I didn't get clear answers to all my questions. It seemed that this was another "condition" in the contract: I had to lay down my own will in the matter and trust God without receiving any definite answer.

Before I left Kansas City I was able to say to the Lord, *If Derek Prince asks me to marry him, I will.* I said that not because I loved Derek Prince, but because I loved the Lord and wanted to please Him. I was "keeping," protecting, my heart.

What a glorious time it was for me in Jerusalem! I stayed in a hospice overlooking the Old City. My room had a balcony where I spent the long evenings. My new surrender to the Lord had brought me into greater intimacy with Him. The Bible was a love letter to me. Three nights between Rosh Hashana and Yom Kippur I stayed awake all night on the balcony. Strangely, I had no need for sleep.

Because my back was stronger, I could take long walks in my beloved city. I kept thanking Jesus for His healing power and presence.

On the day I was to meet Derek at the King David Hotel, I arose early with a song on my lips: "Peace, peace, wonderful peace, coming down from the Father above. . . ." I dressed carefully, and a few minutes before nine walked the short distance to the King David Hotel.

As I walked through the revolving door, Derek rose and came forward to greet me. We shook hands and made our way to the dining room. Breakfast at the King David is a sumptuous buffet, and we made several trips to try the various delicacies. Derek laughed when he saw me taking pickled herring, explaining that he despised it and could never understand Lydia's love for pickled fish. Now he saw I had the same taste.

We chatted about his time in South Africa. Then he reached into his pocket and took out a little box. "I brought you a souvenir from South Africa."

I opened it. Inside was a beautiful tiger's eye brooch, set in gold. It was no small souvenir. *The man is serious,* I thought, paying close attention to everything he said.

Knowing I often attended the synagogue on the Sabbath and holidays, Derek asked if I would like to go that evening for the Kol Nidre service. We went to the Hechal Shlomo, the main synagogue in Jerusalem, and secured two tickets. As we walked out the door, we looked at the tickets. Written in Hebrew, they both said *Prince.*

"I guess you'll have to go as Mrs. Prince," Derek laughed.

My heart skipped a beat. *What is going on?* I asked the Lord. *How fast is he moving?* I received no answer.

As we started down a steep slope, I grasped Derek's arm for momentary support. He didn't let it go! There we were, walking down the street in Jerusalem in broad daylight, arm-in-arm! As soon as I could do so unobtrusively, I disengaged my arm. I had said yes to the Lord, but I wasn't going to be swept off my feet by any man, not even Derek Prince!

Derek gave no indication, however, that our appointment was ending. When we reached the King David again, he asked me formally if I would honor him with my company the rest of the day. I acquiesced, and we found chairs in the shade by the swimming pool.

"Tell me about yourself," he said as we sat down. "Who were your parents? What was your family like? Where did you go to school? I want to know about you. Don't leave anything out."

God gave me tremendous grace. By nature I am an honest person. I may see things from my own vantage point, but I will never distort or deceive. So hour after hour, I told him my story. He asked questions about my ex-husband, my conversion to Judaism, the reasons for the divorce. He was so easy to talk to.

The morning passed. I explained that I followed the Jewish practice of fasting from sunset to sunset on Yom Kippur, and Derek said he would like to join me. Even though we were not hungry after the big breakfast, we decided about two o'clock to go to the dining room for lunch to fortify ourselves for the fast.

As we ate, Derek continued to ply me with questions. Finally I said, "I just can't talk anymore. My strength is running out."

"I was so interested in all you were saying," he apologized. "I didn't realize what a strain it was. I haven't been fair to you."

Then he began to tell me about his struggles after Lydia's death; his search to know God's will for the remainder of his life; his questioning as to whether he should return to Jerusalem, the city he had left in 1948.

Up to this point our conversation had been friendly but a little formal. Now, as he talked, barriers came down and I realized he was divulging his innermost thoughts to me. Most important, he was unconsciously revealing the depth of his personal relationship with the Lord. Although he was a successful Christian leader with great spiritual authority, he looked to the Lord for strength and direction in the same personal way I did!

Then Derek began to tell me why he had invited me, first to
Kansas City and now to the King David. As he described his
final night in Jerusalem in June, I put down my fork and
watched him. Although he was outwardly calm, his voice had
an edge of excitement. His eyes sparkled. He described the
steep hill he had seen in a vision and the woman at its base.

"You were the woman," he concluded, looking at me. "I
understood God was saying that if I am to return to
Jerusalem, the first step is for me to marry you!" He paused,
then added quickly that he did not expect me to respond to
his revelation, but that I must seek the Lord for myself.

I had not noticed how my heart was racing. Now it
quieted. Total inner peace came. Everything fell into place.
To all the questions that had nagged me—why was Derek
Prince interested in me? Why, out of all the women in the
world, had he sought me out? How could he consider a
divorced woman?—I now had the answer.

He was waiting for me to speak. I said simply, "Now I
understand."

"What do you mean?" he exclaimed.

I lowered my eyes. "I thought God was saying you would
ask me to marry you, but I couldn't understand why you
would choose me. You didn't know me or anything about
me. Now I understand. The initiative came from God."

Then I looked into his eyes, and in that moment I loved
him.

I don't think we ever finished lunch. We sat in the lobby.
We walked in the park and sat on a bench overlooking the
Old City. He showed me the diamond he had in his pocket,
wrapped in a piece of white paper. After I went back to my
room at the hospice to rest and change, we had a last cup of
tea before the fast. Then we walked to the synagogue and
separated for the three hours of the service, I to the ladies'
gallery, he to the main floor with the men. He was very

precise as we parted, specifying the exact spot where we would meet outside when the Kol Nidre service ended.

In the gallery, I quieted my heart. I had been swept along on the floodtide through the day. Now I could take stock. I closed my eyes as the familiar Hebrew phrases and melodies rolled over me. Relaxing in the presence of the Lord, I quietly recommitted my life to Him, for His purposes, and now I included, "Even marrying Derek Prince."

Yom Kipper is the most holy day of the Jewish year. Between Rosh Hashana and Yom Kippur, even non-religious Jews usually seek to be reconciled with their neighbors and do good deeds to be assured they are "written in the Book of Life for another year."

There is nothing to compare with Yom Kippur in Jerusalem. All traffic ceases, except for a rare emergency vehicle. There is no radio or television. The whole city is silent. You hear dogs barking, babies crying. There is no traffic to mask the sound. You can even walk in the middle of the street.

As we walked back from the synagogue, now arm-in-arm, Derek said, "I need to say something more to you." We made our way to a bench in the park and sat in the moonlight, the floodlit walls of the Old City before us.

In the stillness of that Yom Kippur eve, Derek said, "You understand I am not free to ask you to marry me yet?"

I nodded. I knew about his relationship with the other teachers.

"We have agreed not to make any major personal decisions without consulting one another," he told me. "I couldn't say anything to them until I knew how you would respond. Now I must consult them. I'll be with them the end of October."

This was September. That was more than a month away! "I'll pray," I responded.

Then we rose and began to walk toward the hospice. Derek looked at me tenderly. "I believe it will be all right," he said.

"Don't be afraid. I believe God has made His will clear to both of us. Let's accept it in faith. I can't offer you breakfast tomorrow, but I invite you to meet me at nine o'clock and we'll spend the day together. I leave early the next day."

That was the beginning of our relationship: a day of solemn prayer and fasting. At the end we committed one another, and our futures, to the Lord, and said our good-byes.

I had many friends in Jerusalem, but no one with whom I could share what had happened on Yom Kippur. As He had been for seven years, Jesus was my only confidant. I poured out my heart to Him and waited for His counsel.

There was nothing mystical about my relationship with Jesus; it was sweet conversation with an intimate friend. I had learned in those years to wait for His direction in my daily life—when and where to go shopping; when to make a phone call; when to undertake tasks. Obedience in these daily matters gave me confidence for the big decisions. Now, after months of semi-invalidism, I was even more dependent on Him. I sought His counsel in all things.

Still unable to sit or stand for any extended period, I could not work. But a large bank transfer from a source in Europe assured me that my heavenly Father was watching to see that I did not lack. I received tapes on spiritual warfare from Derek's meetings in South Africa, which shed new light on my task. I prayed.

As I waited for Derek to meet with the other teachers, we spoke briefly by telephone a few times. Then, early in November, I heard his voice again—but it was flat. The joy and exuberance were gone. He told me they had said no, that they considered it unwise for him to pursue the relationship with me.

With a catch in his voice he added, "I already have my ticket to come to Jerusalem for two days. I will come to tell you personally, and to say good-by." That was all.

I threw myself onto the floor before the Lord and cried, "Why, Lord? Why did You do this to me? Why did You give me such love and then require this of me? I was satisfied with You. I was not seeking a husband. Why did You bring Derek into my life and then do this to me?"

Amazingly, as if His arms were around me, Jesus said, *Trust Me*.

True faith is always on the edge of unbelief. At times I had perfect confidence that God's way was best; at other times I doubted His love and cried out for a fresh sign. Now, on November 13, He gave me what I had prayed and hoped for: a miracle that instantly completed my healing. As I worshiped the Lord in a large public meeting, His power swept through me. Instantly all pain left my body; His strength poured in.

I was lost in worship, in the joy of His presence. After months of continuous agony, alleviated only slightly by medication, to be pain-free was almost like being released from my body!

I was jolted back to earth by a tap on my shoulder. The leaders on the platform had seen me, my face shining, and sent someone to inquire what God was doing. Would I come up and testify?

Transported to the platform by muscles that felt like silk, I stood at the microphone almost speechless, and wept. All over the auditorium filled with tourists—strangers, I could see dear friends from Jerusalem who had prayed for me these seven long months. Their faces glowed as if spotlights were turned on them. I don't remember what I said or how I described what had happened in that moment, but then I looked out at them and said, "Thank you. Thank you, my friends, and thank You, Lord Jesus!"

Later I saw the Lord's wonderful wisdom. By calling me forward to share the miracle, He forced me to make the confession publicly. I believe this really completed my healing. Had I not been confronted with the request to testify, I might have lost my healing the first time I had another twinge of pain.

Some people had said to me during those long months, "Claim your healing." But I could not. Now healing was mine! An occasional twinge did not frighten me because I knew it was part of the process. Later an X-ray showed that God had done more than heal the ruptured disc. He had straightened my curved spine. It was like having a new back!

Four days later I met Derek for breakfast in the King David. His face was ashen; his hands trembled. I wanted to touch him, to comfort him. I prayed silently for him as he spoke. There was nothing else I could do.

He opened his briefcase and took out a letter he handed me, signed by the four teachers. "You understand," he said. "I committed myself to consult them on all major decisions. This is a major decision. I must keep my commitment."

He gave me his itinerary for the next few months, asking me to pray for him as he traveled in ministry. Then, surprisingly, he took out a jar of homemade marmalade, sent to me by his daughter Anna. The inner voice said, *You have a friend.*

The only other thing that brightened our meeting was my report of the miraculous healing of my back. Derek was so grateful to God. He saw that God was taking care of me. Then there was nothing more to say. He put me into a taxi and waved good-by. That was the end of the chapter.

What does a woman do in such a situation? I made myself busy. Stronger each day, able to sit in a chair at last, I re-enrolled in the Hebrew *ulpan.* Six days a week I immersed myself in language study.

I could not share my heartbreak with anyone. In the sleepless nights I wept on the shoulder of Jesus, then rose to smile my way through the day, rejoicing in my healing. I made new friends in my classes and spent time with old friends. I tried not to do too much thinking or speculating. And I prayed. I spent hours, nights, weeks, praying, fasting, interceding—not only for Derek, but for Israel and for the Jewish people. President Sadat of Egypt came to Jerusalem the day after Derek left. On every street corner people talked of "peace at last!" It was a critical time. Praying for Israel kept my mind off myself.

But it was not easy. I had promised to obey the Lord as I heard His voice. I had opened my heart to Derek because I believed that was God's will. Jesus had broken the hard shell I had built around it in 1965. Only now did I realize how vulnerable I had become.

I had two choices: I could harden my heart again and never let anyone close to me. Or I could trust Jesus to heal my broken heart as He had healed my injured back.

I made my choice. Proverbs 3:5–6 became my confession. I determined to trust in the Lord with all my heart. I would not try to understand. I would acknowledge Him in all my ways. I would trust Him to direct my paths.

As I followed Derek's itinerary with my prayers, a strange thing happened: Despair left and hope came. There would be another chapter. One week in particular stood out, while Derek was in Adelaide, Australia. One day as I was in class, tears began to roll down my face. Embarrassed, I excused myself. After composing myself in the ladies' room, I boarded the bus to go home. Again, uncontrollable tears. Weeping in my room, I began to pray in tongues. Hours went by, the burden never lifting.

This was not a new phenomenon for me. I had experienced such travail in the Spirit numerous times in connection with Israel, both before and after I immigrated. I seldom knew the cause until afterward—a terrorist raid, a crisis in the government, the beginning of war. This time I knew it was connected with Derek.

Three days later I wrote in my journal, "Thank God, Adelaide is over!" I sensed something had broken in the spiritual world.

Early spring came to Jerusalem. I moved to a one-room flat in the center of the city. Then a telegram came: "Coming to Jerusalem with a Lutheran tour. Meet me in the King David for breakfast." This was the new chapter!

When we met, I saw instantly that Derek had also been meeting with the Lord. There was a new gentleness in his voice, a brokenness in his whole demeanor. We served ourselves at the buffet and chatted as the waiter brought our tea. Then, characteristically, Derek came to the point: "I prayed it through in Adelaide. I still believe it is God's will for us to marry. Has He shown you anything?"

I told him of my experience the week he was in Adelaide and my unexpected, unexplainable hope. We marveled at the Holy Spirit's working. Separated by the greatest distance on earth, we had prayed in one accord.

In faith, believing God would work things out, we took this time to get better acquainted. As we walked all over Jerusalem, Derek commented enthusiastically on my strength and agility. He had met me as an invalid; now I was active and energetic. Together we visited with spiritual leaders in Jerusalem who were my personal friends. I knew he was "checking me out," watching to see how I related to them, what their attitudes were toward me.

One day we met an elderly Christian woman who had lived in the city for many years, an ardent admirer of Derek's. Taking in the situation at a glance, she began to prophesy: "God has been observing you. You were an exemplary husband to Lydia. You deserve the best. He has given Ruth to you."

Derek thanked her, but cautioned her that nothing was settled. "My lips are sealed!" she said, and off she went as abruptly as she had appeared.

When Derek returned to the U.S., where he would again meet with the other teachers, I returned to my studies. But it was spring. My heart was light. It was hard to concentrate. Then Derek phoned me, his voice jubilant. The other teachers had also been praying, and God had given them a new perspective. Derek would be bringing a tour out to Israel in April. We would make our plans. He was not yet ready, he told me, to make the move to Jerusalem, and he asked me to leave for a time until God made it plain that we should settle there.

When I met Derek at Ben Gurion Airport, it was the beginning of a new phase of my life. I had been an anonymous Jewish believer living in Jerusalem. Now I was thrust into the limelight of the charismatic world. As soon as we announced our engagement to a small group of Derek's close friends, the tour members focused their attention on us. They photographed us everywhere we went. One woman walked up to me as we stood in line waiting to eat lunch and said, "I heard Derek Prince is getting married again. Are you *it?*" I smilingly conceded I was *it.*

Before Derek departed for the U.S., we went to a vantage point overlooking Jerusalem. Gazing out over the city, we reflected on all that God had done. Then we prayed, "Lord, settle us in Jerusalem in Your way and time."

I prayed that prayer with mixed emotions. It was another death for me, a laying down of my will. Jerusalem was much more than the city in which I lived; it was the city to which God had specifically called me, and my love for it was God-given. But my love for Derek was God-given, too. I had to trust God to work the two together in His way and time. I understood clearly that the bride must leave her home and go to the home provided by her bridegroom.

While it was hard to leave Jerusalem, it was no sacrifice to go to be with Derek. Although we had had only a few days together at widely spaced intervals, the Holy Spirit was joining us with ever-deepening bonds. Laying down our relationship and letting it die had driven each of us into the Lord, making us more dependent on Him. Because we had touched the Lord in our brokenness, we now had more to give to one another. We treasured every moment together.

In June I left Jerusalem for Florida. Derek had the South African diamond set into a ring for my finger. (We call it the "Faith Diamond" because Derek bought it in faith for a woman he scarcely knew.)

Our marriage during the Jewish Feast of Tabernacles blended the Jewish and Christian traditions. Charles Simpson performed the ceremony and the other teachers laid hands on us and blessed us. What a glorious celebration! We returned to Jerusalem for our honeymoon, and a few months later to study Hebrew at the university. Being married to Derek *and* being in Jerusalem, seemed like a wonderful dream. The Lord began there to lead us into intercession together, with power far exceeding our individual prayer lives.

Now it became clear to me that my whole life had been preparation to be Derek's wife. Derek is a friend of the Jewish people and committed to the restoration of the State of Israel. Twenty-five years earlier, God had taken me into Judaism. My identification with the Jewish people and my understanding of their customs and traditions are an invaluable asset to him.

In my years in Jerusalem, I had come to know the city like my back garden—the shops, the parks, the quiet little streets. I had also learned much of the culture of the Middle East, so different from America or Britain—Jewish ways of thinking, customs, viewpoints, business practices. Derek, returning to a totally changed city after thirty years, commented that God had provided him with his own personal guide!

Until I came to Jerusalem, I had never been out of the U.S., although I had traveled extensively within its borders. My years in this cosmopolitan city helped prepare me for the various situations and cultures I would encounter in our traveling ministry.

As I see it, my primary responsibility is to surround Derek with a quiet and peaceful atmosphere so that he can bring out all that God has put into him. Lydia invested all her spiritual knowledge, wisdom, and experience in him. As she grew older, Derek cared for her. Now I invest myself in him—caring for him, protecting him from unnecessary interruptions and distractions, helping him in every possible way so that he is free to seek the Lord and bring forth fresh, anointed, prophetic teaching to the Body of Christ. This is true whether we are in our home in Jerusalem, at our base in Florida, or traveling for several months at a time. It requires a diversity of skills acquired over a lifetime.

Most important of all, God has taken me through suffering, illness, tests, heartbreak, and a life of prayer and intercession—as difficult as these were for a woman alone—into a depth of dependence on the Holy Spirit that embraces every area of my life. That dependence enables me to blend my thoughts and personality with Derek's, without endangering the integrity of my own personality. I think I understand what Adam meant when he said that Eve was "bone of my bones and flesh of my flesh" (Genesis 2:23). I rely on the Holy Spirit to show me when to be available to Derek and when to withdraw, when to speak and when to be silent, when to submit and when to express my own point of view, when to seek his opinion and when to use my own judgment.

The supernatural gift of faith that God gave me in the beginning, coupled with the trust that came through seven years of walking with Him, prepared me for the magnitude of responsibility as Derek's wife. "Without faith it is impossible to please God" (Hebrews 11:6), and without faith it would be impossible to be Derek's wife.

When we married, he took me into full partnership in Derek Prince Ministries. It was a modest operation, making cassettes and publishing his books, employing a dozen people. Since then, the expansion of the ministry has been dramatic. It seems as if God could not release His full plan for the ministry until He had provided Derek with me as his helper.

Three months after our marriage, Derek commenced his radio program, *Today with Derek Prince*. By 1985 it circled the globe, including translations that reach all of Communist China in their three main dialects: Mandarin, Cantonese, Amoy. The Spanish version is broadcast to all of South and Central America, and a Russian translation is being prepared.

Derek's materials, which sell widely in many languages in the Western world, go out free of charge through our Global Outreach program to those who have no means to pay. Christian leaders in remote third world areas and behind the Iron Curtain transmit this teaching in turn to their own people in their own languages. Branch offices of Derek Prince Ministries have been opened in the United Kingdom, South Africa, Australia, and New Zealand.

The little stream has become a river; the river has become a sea; the sea is becoming a mighty ocean. God joined Derek and Lydia together in the same yoke and harness to do the plowing and the sowing. Now, in Derek's later years, God has joined me to Derek to bring God's full plan for his life to fruition and to share with him in the reaping.

In our marriage ceremony, Derek bestowed his name on me and vowed to share freely all that God gives him of honor, authority, and possessions. I hold all these in high esteem, knowing that one day I will be accountable to God for all I have received. "[To whom] much is given, of him shall be much required" (Luke 12:8, KJV). My confident assurance is that I am pleasing the Lord in the way I serve Derek and his ministry.

And my confident response to young people today who desire ardently to marry, and who doubt God's love for them because they have no mate, is from Psalm 37:4: "Delight yourself in the Lord and He will give you the desires of your heart."